Welcome! Isten hozta!

Titles in this series:

Just Enough **Hungarian**

D. L. Ellis, A. Cheyne

PASSPORT BOOKS
a division of *NTC Publishing Group*
Lincolnwood, Illinois USA

First Published in 1992 by Passport Books,
a division of NTC Publishing Group,
4255 West Touhy Avenue,
Lincolnwood (Chicago), Illinois 60646-1975 U.S.A.
in conjunction with Corvina Publishing Company,
Budapest, Hungary and Pan Books, U.K.
Manufactured in the United States of America.

8 9 AG 9 8 7 6 5 4

Contents

Using the phrase book

- Though primarily designed to help you get by in Hungary, to get what you want or need, this phrase book would also be of use to travelers to Hungary in general. It concentrates on the simplest but most effective way you can express these needs in an unfamiliar language.
- The CONTENTS on *p. 5.* give you a good idea of which section to consult for the phrase you need.
- The INDEX on *p. 145.* gives more detailed information about where to look for your phrase.
- When you have found the right page you will be given:
  either — the exact phrase
  or — help in making up a suitable sentence
  and — help to get the pronunciation right.
- The sentences in **bold type** will be useful for you in a variety of different situations, so they are worth learning by heart. (*See* also DO IT YOURSELF, *p. 137.*)
- Wherever possible you will find help in understanding what Hungarian-speaking people say to *you*, in reply to your questions.
- If you want to practise the basic nuts and bolts of the language further, look at the DO IT YOURSELF section starting on *p. 137.*
- Note especially these three sections:
  — Everyday expressions *p. 12.*
  — Shop talk *p. 56.*
  — Public notices *p. 117.*
  You are sure to want to refer to them most frequently.
- Once abroad, remember to make good use of the local tourist offices (*see p. 25.*).

US addresses:
Hungarian Consulate
8 East 75th Street
New York, N.Y. 10021
ph. (212) 879-4127

IBUSZ (Hungarian Travel Bureau)
630 Fifth Avenue, New York,
Rockefeller Center — Suite 2455
ph. (212) 582-7412

MALÉV (Hungarian Airlines)
630 Fifth Avenue, New York,
Rockefeller Center — Room 1900
ph. (212) 757-6480, 757-6481, 757-6446, (800) 223-6884
fax (212) 459-0675

1888 Century Park East 410
Los Angeles, CA. 90067
ph. (213) 286-7980
fax (213) 286-1921

111 East Wacker Drive, Suite 306
Los Angeles
ph. (312) 819-5353
(800) 877-5429
fax (312) 819-5355

Addresses in Great Britain:

Hungarian Consulate
35 Eaton Place
London S.W.1.
ph. (71) 235-2664

IBUSZ (Hungarian Travel Bureau)
6 Conduit Street
London W1R 9T6
ph. (71) 493-0263

MALÉV (Hungarian Airlines)
10 Vigo Street
London S.W.1.
ph. (71) 439-0577, 439-0578
Heathrow Airport
ph. (71) 745-7093, 897-0461

Australian addresses:

Hungarian Consulate
Sydney, Unit 6.
351a Edgecliff Road
Edgecliff N.S.W. 2027
ph. (2) 328-7860, 328-7859

Useful addresses in Hungary:

Embassy of the United States
Budapest, V.
Szabadság tér 12.
ph. (1) 112-6450

Embassy of Australia
Budapest, VI.
Délibáb u. 30.
ph. (1) 153-4233

Embassy of the United Kingdom
Budapest, V.
Harmincad u. 6.
ph. (1) 118-2888

A note on the pronunciation system

In traveler's phrase books there is usually a pronunciation section which tries to teach English-speaking tourists how to correctly pronounce the language of the country they are visiting. This is based on the belief that in order to be understood, the speaker must have an accurate, authentic accent — that he must pronounce every last word letter — perfectly.

The authors of this book on the other hand, wanted to devise a workable and usable pronunciation system. So they had to face the fact it is absolutely impossible for an average speaker of English who has no technical training in phonetics and phonetic transcription systems (which includes 98% of all users of this book!) to reproduce the sounds of a foreign language with perfect accuracy, just from reading a phonetic transcription, cold — no prior background in the language. We also believe that you don't have to have perfect pronunciation in order to make yourself understood in a foreign country. After all, natives you run into will take into account that you are foreigners, and visitors, and more than likely they will feel gratified by your efforts to communicate and will probably go out of their way to try to understand you. They may even help you, and correct you, in a friendly manner. We have found, also, that visitors to a foreign country are not usually concerned with perfect pronunciation — they just want to get their message across, to communicate!

With this in mind we have designed a pronunciation system which is of the utmost simplicity to use. This system does not attempt to give an accurate — but also problematical and tedious — representation of the sound system of the language, but instead uses common sound and letter combinations in English which are the closest to the sounds in the foreign language. In this way, the sentences transcribed for pronunciation should be read as naturally as possible, as if they were ordinary English. In no way does the user have to attempt to make the words sound "foreign". So, while to yourself you will sound as if you are speaking ordinary English — or at least making ordinary English sounds — you will at the same time be making yourselves understood in another language. And, as the saying goes, practice makes perfect, so it is probably a good idea to repeat aloud to yourselves several times the phrases you think you are going to use, before you actually use them. This will give you greater confidence, and will also help in making yourself understood.

A few things to remember though:
— in Hungarian stress always falls on the first syllable of the word,
— in Hungarian there exist no „mute" vowels; even final vowels are fully pronounced,
— in Hungarian double length in the case of consonants is shown by doubling the letter, or where the sound is represented by two letters (letter combination) by doubling the first,
— short hyphens in the phonetic respelling are used to mark off compound words or verbal prefixes, or to break longer words into more easily pronounced segments,
— "r" should be pronounced always rolled, as in Scots,
— there are a few sounds (and corresponding letter combinations) that are rather unfamiliar to an English ear (or eye) even in our respelling:

dj should be pronounced	as in *due*
nj	as in *new*
ö/ő	as in *bird, herd*

Of course you may enjoy trying to pronounce a foreign language as well as possible and the present system is a good way to start. However, since it uses only the sounds of English, you will very soon need to depart from it as you imitate the sounds you hear the native speaker produce and begin to relate them to the spelling of the other language. Hungarian will pose no problem as there is an obvious and consistent relationship between pronunciation and spelling; each letter or combination of letters always has the same sound value.

Jó szórakozást!

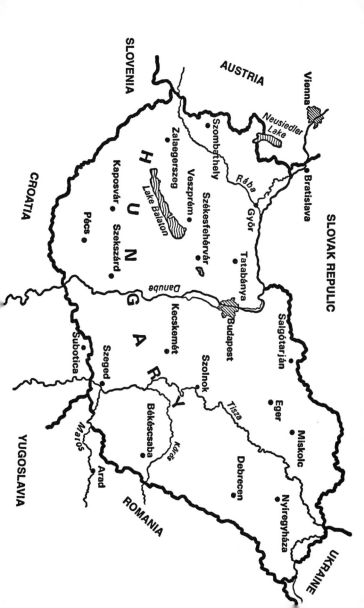

Everyday expressions

(See also "Shop talk", p. 56.)

Hello	**Szervusz** (familiar)
	ser-voos
Good morning	**Jó reggelt**
	yow raig-gailt
Good day/Good afternoon	**Jó napot**
	yow naw-pot
Good evening	**Jó estét**
	yow esh-tayt
Good night	**Jó éjszakát**
	yow ey-so-kaat
Good-bye	**Viszontlátásra**
	vee-sont-laa-taash-roh
	Szervusz
	ser-voos
See you later	**Viszontlátásra**
	vee-sont-laa-taash-roh
Yes	**Igen**
	ee-ghen
Please	**Kérem**
	kay-rem
Yes, please	**Igen, kérem**
	ee-gain, kay-rem
Great!	**Nagyszerű**
	nodj-seh-rooh
Thank you	**Köszönöm**
	kö-sö-nöm
Thank you very much	**Köszönöm szépen**
	kö-sö-nöm say-pen
That's right	**Úgy van**
	oodj von
No	**Nem**
	nem
No, thank you	**Nem, köszönöm**
	nem, kö-sö-nöm
I disagree	**Nem értek egyet**
	nem air-tek ed-yet
Excuse me	**Bocsásson meg**
Sorry	bow-chaash-shon megh

Don't mention it/That's OK	**Nem tesz semmit**
	nem tess shem-meet
That's good/I like it	**Ez tetszik**
	ez tet-seek
That's no good/I don't like it	**Ez nem tetszik**
	ez nem tet-seek
I know	**Tudom**
	toodom
I don't know	**Nem tudom**
	nem toodom
It doesn't matter	**Nem számít**
	nem saam-eet
Where is the toilet, please?	**Hol van a WC, kérem?**
	hol von o vey-tsey, kay-rem?
How much is that?	**Mennyibe kerül ez?**
	men-yee-beh ke-rool ez?
Is the service included?	**A kiszolgálás benne van?**
	o kee-sol-golosh ben-neh von?
Do you speak English?	**Beszél angolul?**
	be-sail on-gow-lool?
I'm sorry...	**Sajnos...**
	shoy-nosh...
I don't speak Hungarian	**nem beszélek magyarul**
	nem beh-sailek mod-yor-ool
I only speak a little Hungarian	**csak egy kicsit beszélek magyarul**
	chok edj kee-cheet beh-sailek mod-yor-oohl
I don't understand	**nem értem**
	nem air-tem
Please, can you...	**Kérem...**
	kay-rem ...
repeat that?	**meg tudná ezt ismételni**
	megh tood-noh est ish-may-telny
speak more slowly?	**nem tudna lassabban beszélni?**
	nem tood-noh losh-shob-bon be-sail-ny?
write that down?	**le tudná ezt írni?**
	leh tood-nah est eer-ny?
What is this called in Hungarian?	**Hogy hívják ezt magyarul?**
	hodj heev-yaak est mod-yor-ool

Crossing the border

ESSENTIAL INFORMATION

- Don't waste time just before you leave rehearsing what you are going to say to the border officials — the chances are that you won't have to say anything at all, especially if you travel by air.
- It's more useful to check that you have your documents handy for the journey: passport, tickets, money, traveler's checks, insurance documents, driving licence and car registration documents.
- Look out for these signs:
  VÁM (customs)
  HATÁR (border)
  HATÁRŐRSÉG (frontier police)
  [For further signs and notices, see p. 117.]
- You may be asked routine questions by the customs officials *[see below]*. If you have to give personal details see "Meeting people", *p. 16*. The other important answer to know is "Nothing": **Semmi** (shem-mee).

ROUTINE QUESTIONS

Passport?	**Útlevél?**
	oot-leh-vail?
Insurance?	**Biztosítás?**
	biz-towsh-eet-aash?
Registration document (logbook)	**Forgalmi engedély?**
	fowr-goal-mee en-geh-day?
Have you anything to declare?	**Van valami elvámolnivalója?**
	von vo-lo-mee el-vaa-molny vo-low-yah?
Where are you going?	**Hová utazik?**
	how-voh oot-ozeek?
How long are you staying?	**Meddig marad?**
	med-digh mo-rod?
Where have you come from?	**Honnan jön?**
	hown-non yön?

You may also have to fill in forms which ask for:

surname	**Vezetéknév**
first name	**Utónév**
maiden name	**Leánykori név**
place of birth	**Születési hely**
date of birth yr/mo/d	**Születési év/hónap/nap**
address	**Lakcím**
nationality	**Állampolgárság**
profession	**Foglalkozás**
passport number	**Útlevélszám**
issued at	**Kiállítás helye**
signature	**Aláírás**

Meeting people

[See also "Everyday expressions" p. 12.]

Breaking the ice

Hello	**Jó napot** yow nop-pot
Good morning	**Jó reggelt** yow reg-gelt
How are you?	**Hogy van? (Hogy vagy?)** hodj von? (hodj vodj?)

[Expressions above in brackets should only be used with people you know well.]

Pleased to meet you	**Örülök, hogy megismerkedhettem Önnel** ö-roo-lök, hodj meg-eesh-mer-ked-het-tem Ön-nel
I am here...	**... vagyok itt** ... vod-yok eet
on holiday	**turistaúton** toor-eeshtoh-oot-on
on business	**üzleti úton** ooz-lety oot-on
Can I offer you ...	**Megkínálhatom egy...** meg-keen-ol-hotowm edj...
a drink?	**itallal?** eet-ol-lol?
a cigarette?	**cigarettával?** tsee-go-ret-taa-vol?
a cigar?	**szivarral?** see-vor-rol?
Are you staying long?	**Sokáig marad?** sho-kaah-ig mo-rod?

Name

What's your name?	**Mi az Ön neve?** mee oz ön neh-veh?
My name is ...	**Az én nevem ...** oz ain neh-vem ...

Family

Are you married?	**Ön nős? (Mr)**
	ön nösh?
	Ön férjezett? (Mrs)
	ön fair-yeh-zett?
I am ...	
married	**nős vagyok (Mr)**
	nösh vod-yok
	asszony vagyok (Mrs)
	os-sonj vod-yok
single	**nőtlen vagyok (Mr)**
	nöt-len vod-yok
	nincs férjem (Miss)
	ninch fair-yem
This is...	**Bemutatom...**
	beh-moot-otom
my wife	**a feleségemet**
	aw feh-leh-shaigemet
my husband	**a férjemet**
	aw fair-yemet
my son	**a fiamat**
	aw fee-yomot
my daughter	**a lányomat**
	aw laanj-omot
my (boy)friend	**a barátomat**
	aw bor-aat-omot
my (girl)friend	**a barátnőmet**
	aw boraat-nöh-met
my colleague	**a kollégámat**
	aw kowl-laig-aamot
Do you have any children?	**Vannak gyerekei?**
	von-nok djereh-keh-eeh?
I have...	**Van...**
	von...
one daughter	**egy lányom**
	edj laanj-owm
one son	**egy fiam**
	edj fee-yom
two daughters	**két lányom**
	kait laanj-owm
three sons	**három fiam**
	haa-rom fee-yom

No, I haven't any children   **Nem, nincsenek gyerekeim**
nem, ninchenek djereh-keh-eem

Where do you live?

Are you Hungarian?   **Ön magyar?**
ön modjor

I am American   **Amerikai vagyok**
oh-meh-ree-koh-ee vodjok

I am English   **Angol vagyok**
on-gohl vodjok

[For other nationalities, see p. 129.]

Where are you from?

I'm from Pécs   **Pécsi vagyok**
paichy vodjok

I'm from Hungary   **Magyarországról jöttem**
modjor-or-saag-rowl jöt-tem

I'm from the south   **Délről jöttem**
dail-röl jöt-tem

I'm from the north   **Északról jöttem**
aisok-rowl jöt-tem

I'm from the east   **Keletről jöttem**
kelet-röl jöt-tem

I'm from the west   **Nyugatról jöttem**
njoog-ot-rowl jöt-tem

[For other countries, see p. 129.]

For the businessman and businesswoman

I'm from... (firm's name)   **A (firm's name)-től vagyok**
o (firm's name)-töl vodjok

I have an appointment with...   **Találkozóm van ... úrral (Mr)**
tolaal-koh-zowm von ... oor-rol
Találkozóm van
    ... asszonnyal (Mrs/Miss)
tolaal-koh-zowm von
... osson-yol

May I speak to...?	**Beszélhetnék ... úrral? (Mr)** besail-het-naik ... oor-rol? **Beszélhetnék ... asszonnyal? (Mrs/Miss)** besail-het-naik ... osson-yol?
This is my card	**Ez a névjegyem** ez o naiv-yedjem
I'm sorry, I'm late	**Sajnos elkéstem kicsit** shoy-nosh el-kaish-tem kicheet
Can I fix another appointment?	**Megbeszélhetnénk egy másik találkozót?** meg-besail-het-naink moh-shik to-laal-kozowt?
I'm staying at the (Crown) hotel I'm staying in (Park) Road	**A (Korona) hotelben lakom** o (ko-ro-no) hotel-ben lo-kom **A (Park) utcában lakom** o (park) ut-saa-bon lo-kom

Asking the way

ESSENTIAL INFORMATION

- Keep a lookout for all these place names as you will find them on shops, maps and notices.

WHAT TO SAY

Excuse me, please

Bocsásson meg, kérem
bow-chaash-shown meg, kay-rem

How do I get...
to Budapest?

Hogy jutok el...
   Budapestre?
hodj yootok el
boodoh-peshtre?

to (Station) Road?

az (Állomás) utcába?
oz (aal-lomaash) ootsah-bah?

to the hotel (Korona)?

a (Korona) hotelbe?
aw (kow-rowna) hotel-beh?

to the airport?

a repülőtérre?
aw reh-poolow-tair-reh?

to the beach?

a partra?
aw part-rah?

to the bus station?

a buszmegállóba?
aw boos-meg-aal-low-bah?

to the historic site?

a történelmi emlékhelyre?
aw tör-tainel-mee emlaik-hey-reh?

to the market?

a piacra?
aw pee-ots-rah?

to the police station?

a rendőrségre?
aw rendör-shaig-reh?

to the port?

a kikötőbe?
aw kee-kötöh-beh?

to the post office?

a postára?
aw posh-taah-roh?

to the railway station?

a pályaudvarra?
aw paayoh-oodvor-roh?

to the sports stadium?

a stadionba?
aw shtody-own-boh?

to the tourist information office?	**az idegenforgalmi hivatalba?** oz eedeghen-fowr-gholmy khee-vaah-taal-bah?
to the town center?	**a városközpontba?** aw vaarosh-kös-pont-boh?
to the town hall?	**a városházára?** aw vaarosh-haaz-zaah-roh?
Excuse me, please	**Bocsásson meg kérem** bow-chaash-shown meg, kay-rem
Is there ... nearby?	**Van itt ... a közelben?** von eet ... aw köh-zel-ben?
an art gallery	**képtár** kaip-taar
a baker's	**pék** paik
a bank	**bank** bonk
a bar	**bár** baar
a botanical garden	**botanikus kert** bowt-ony-koosh kert
a bus stop	**buszmegálló** boos-meg-aal-low
a butcher's	**hentes** hen-tesh
a café	**eszpresszó** es-pres-sow
a cake shop	**cukrászda** tsook-raas-dow
a campsite	**kemping** kem-ping
a car park	**parkoló** park-ow-low
a change bureau	**pénzváltó** painz-vaal-tow
a chemist's	**háztartási bolt** khaaz-thar-taashe bolt
a church	**templom** tem-plowm
a cinema	**mozi** mow-zee
a delicatessen	**csemege üzlet** cheh-meh-geh ooz-let

a dentist's	**fogászat**
	fowg-aas-ot
a department store	**áruház**
	aaroo-haaz
a disco	**diszkó**
	dees-kow
a doctor's surgery	**orvosi rendelő**
	owr-vowshy rendeh-lö
a dry cleaner's	**tisztító**
	tees-tee-taw
a fishmonger's	**halas**
	ho-losh
a garage (for repairs)	**autószerelő**
	oh-ootow-sereh-lö
a hairdresser's	**fodrász**
	fowd-raas
a greengrocer's	**zöldséges**
	zöld-shaig-esh
a grocer's	**közért**
	köz-airt
a hardware shop	**vas és edény üzlet**
	vosh aish ed-ainj ooz-let
a hospital	**kórház**
	kowr-haaz
a hotel	**szálloda**
	saal-low-doh
an ice-cream parlor	**fagylaltozó**
	fodj-lol-tow-zow
a local sickness insurance office	**betegbiztosító iroda**
	beteg-bees-towshee-tow eerow-doh
a laundry	**mosoda**
	moshow-doh
a museum	**múzeum**
	mooz-eh-oom
a newsagent's	**újságos**
	ooy-shaa-gosh
a night club	**bár**
	baahr
a park	**park**
	powrk
a gas station	**benzinkút**
	ben-zeen-koot

a mailbox	**postaláda**
	powshtah-laah-dow
a public telephone	**telefonfülke**
	teleh-fown-fool-keh
a public toilet	**nyilvános vécé**
	njeel-vaanosh vey-tsey
a restaurant	**étterem**
	ait-terem
a snack bar	**bisztró**
	bees-trow
a sports ground	**sportpálya**
	shpowrt-paa-yoh
a supermarket	**ABC-áruház**
	ah-bey-tsey aah-roo-haaz
a sweet shop	**édességbolt**
	aidesh-shaig-bowlt
a swimming pool	**uszoda**
	oosow-doh
a taxi stand	**taxiállomás**
	tok-see-aal-low-maash
a theater	**színház**
	seen-haaz
a tobacconist's	**trafik**
	tro-feek
a travel agent's	**utazási iroda**
	ootoz-aashy eerow-doh
a youth hostel	**diákszálló**
	dee-aak-saal-low
a zoo	**állatkert**
	aal-lot-kert

DIRECTIONS

- Asking where a place is, or if a place is near by, is one thing; making sense of the answer is another.
- Here are some of the most important key directions and replies.

Left	**Balra**
	bol-rah
Right	**Jobbra**
	yowb-rah

Straight on	**Egyenesen**
	edjen-eshen
There	**Ott**
	awt
First left/right	**Első utca balra/jobbra**
	el-show oot-soh bol-roh/yowb-rah
Second left/right	**Második utca balra/jobbra**
	maash-owdeek oot-soh ...
At the crossroads	**A kereszteződésnél**
	aw keres-tezow-daish-nail
At the traffic lights	**A jelzőlámpánál**
	aw yel-zow-laam-paah-naal
At the roundabout	**A körforgalomnál**
	aw kör-fowr-gowlom-naal
At the grade-crossing	**A vasúti átjárónál**
	aw vow-shooty aat-yaarow-naal
It's near/far	**Közel/messze van**
	kö-zel/mes-seh von
One kilometer	**Egy kilométer**
	edj keelow-maiter
Two kilometers	**Két kilométer**
	kait keelow-maiter
Five minutes ...	**Öt perc ...**
	öt perts ...
on foot	**gyalog**
	djoh-lowg
by car	**autóval**
	oh-ootow-vol
Take ...	**Menjen ...**
	men-yen
the bus	**busszal**
	boos-sol
the train	**vonattal**
	vow-not-tol
the tram	**villamossal**
	veel-lawmosh-shol
the subway	**metróval**
	metrow-vol

[For public transport, see p. 108.]

The tourist information office

ESSENTIAL INFORMATION

- Most towns and holiday resorts in Hungary have a tourist information office; in smaller towns the local travel agent (**utazási iroda**) provides the same information and services.
- Look for these words:
  IDEGENFORGALMI HIVATAL
  IBUSZ
  TOURINFORM
- If your main concern is to find and book accommodation, an **IBUSZ**-office (the largest travel agency — eeboos) is the best place to go to. Ask for **SZOBAFOGLALÁS** — sowboh-fow-glolaash; but most probably you'll be understood in English.
- Tourist offices offer you free information in the form of printed leaflets, foldouts, brochures, lists and plans.
- You may have to pay for some types of documents.
- For finding a tourist office, see p. 20.

WHAT TO SAY

Please, have you got...	**Kérem, van önnek ...**
	kay-rem, von ön-nek
a plan of the town?	**várostérképe?**
	vaarosh-tair-kaipeh?
a list of events?	**eseménynaptára?**
	esheh-mainj-nop-taaroh?
a list of hotels?	**listája a szállodákról?**
	leeshtaa-ya aw saal-low-daak-rowl?
a list of campsites?	**listája a kempingekről?**
	leeshtaa-ya aw kem-pingek-röl?
a list of restaurants?	**listája az éttermekről?**
	leeshtaa-ya oz ait-termek-röl?
a list of coach excursions?	**listája a buszkirándulásokról?**
	leeshtaa-ya aw boos-keeraan-doolaashok-rowl?
a leaflet on the town?	**prospektusa a városról?**
	prosh-pektoosh-oh aw vaarosh-rowl?

a leaflet on the region?	**prospektusa a környékről?** prosh-pektoosh-oh aw kör-njaik-röl
a railway timetable?	**vasúti menetrendje?** vosh-shooty menet-rend-yeh?
a bus timetable?	**buszmenetrendje?** boos-menet-rend-yeh?
In English, please	**Angolul, kérem** ongowl-lool, kay-rem
How much do I owe you?	**Mennyivel tartozom?** menjee-vel tor-tow-zom?
Can you recommend a cheap hotel?	**Tudna egy olcsó szállodát ajánlani?** tood-nah edj owl-chow saal-low-daat oyaan-lo-nee?
Can you recommend a cheap restaurant?	**Tudna egy olcsó vendéglőt ajánlani?** tood-nah edj owl-chow ven-daig-löt oyaan-lo-nee?
Can you make a booking for me?	**Foglalna nekem egy szobát?** fowg-lol-noh nekem edj sow-baat?

LIKELY ANSWERS

You need to understand when the answer is "No". You should be able to tell by the assistant's facial expression, tone of voice and gesture, but there are some language clues, such as:

No	**Nem** nem
I'm sorry	**Sajnálom** shoy-naal-om
I don't have a list of campsites	**Nincsen listám a kempingekről** neenchen leesh-taam aw kem-pingek-röl
I haven't got any left	**Nincs több/elfogyott** neench töb/el-fow-djott
It's free	**Ingyen van** een-djen von

Accommodation

Hotel

ESSENTIAL INFORMATION

- If you want hotel-type accommodation, all the following words in capital letters are worth looking for on name boards:
  HOTEL
  SZÁLLODA
  MOTEL
  PANZIÓ (boardinghouse)
  SZOBA KIADÓ or very often in German: **ZIMMER FREI** (rooms to let in private houses, bed and breakfast)
- A list of hotels in the town or district can usually be obtained at the local tourist information office *[see p. 25.]*
- Unlisted hotels are cheaper.
- Not all hotels and boardinghouses provide meals apart from breakfast; inquire about this, on arrival at the reception.
- The cost is usually displayed in the room itself, so you can check it when having a look round before agreeing to stay.
- Ask if the displayed cost is for the room itself, per night or per person. It usually includes service charges and taxes, but quite often doesn't include breakfast.
- Breakfast is continental style, with rolls, butter and jam; boiled eggs, cheese and cold meats are usually available on request. Some larger hotels also offer a **SVÉDASZTAL** — shvaid-ostol (breakfast buffet) where you can help yourself to cereals, yoghurt, fresh fruit, etc.
- Resort hotels usually offer full board (**TELJES PENZIÓ** — tel-yesh penzee-ow) of breakfast, lunch and dinner for a set price.
- Upon arrival you will have to fill in the official registration form which bears an English translation. The receptionist will also want to see your passport.
- It is customary to tip the porter.
- Finding a hotel, see *p. 20.*

WHAT TO SAY

I have a booking	**Szobafoglalásom van** sow-boh-fowg-loh-laashom von
Have you any vacancies, please?	**Van üres szobájuk, kérem?** von ooresh sow-boh-yook, kay-rem?
Can I book a room?	**Foglalhatnék szobát?** fowg-lol-hot-naik sow-baat?

It's for ...

one person	**egy személyre** edj semay-reh
two people	**két személyre** kait semay-reh

[For numbers, see p. 121.]

It's for one night	**egy éjszakára** edj aysaw-kaw-roh
It's for two nights	**két éjszakára** kait aysaw-kaw-roh
It's for one week	**egy hétre** edj hait-reh
It's for two weeks	**két hétre** kait hait-reh

I would like ...   **Szeretnék ...**
seret-naik

a room	**egy szobát** edj sow-baat
two rooms	**két szobát** kait sow-baat
a room with a single bed	**egyágyas szobát** edj-aadjosh sow-baat
a room with two single beds	**kétágyas szobát** kait-aadjosh sow-baat

I would like a room ...   **Szeretnék egy szobát ...**
seret-naik edj sow-baat ...

with a bathroom	**fürdőszobával** foordö-sowbaa-vol
with a shower	**zuhanyozóval** zoohonj-owzow-vol
with a cot	**pótággyal** powt-aadj-djol
with a balcony	**erkéllyel** er-kay-yel

I would like ...	**Szeretnék ...** seret-naik ...
full board	**teljes penziót** tel-yesh penzee-owt
half board	**félpenziót** fail-penzee-owt
bed and breakfast	**csak reggelit** chok reg-gheleet
[See Essential Information]	
Do you serve meals?	**Van melegkonyhájuk?** von melegh-kownj-haa-yook?
At what time is ... breakfast?	**Mikor van ...?** **reggeli?** reg-ghelee?
lunch?	**ebéd?** eh-baid?
dinner?	**vacsora?** vo-chow-roh?
How much is it?	**Mibe kerül?** mee-beh keh-rool?
Can I look at the room?	**Megnézhetném a szobát?** meg-naiz-hetnaim aw sow-baat?
I'd prefer a room ...	**Olyan szobát szeretnék, amelyik ...** oy-on sow-baat seret-naik, omeh-yeek ...
at the front	**az utcára néz ...** oz oot-saaroh naiz ...
at the back	**az udvarra néz ...** oz oodvor-roh naiz ...
OK, I'll take it	**Ez megfelel** ez megfelel
No thanks, I won't take it	**Ez nem felel meg** ez nem felel meg
The key to number (10), please	**A (tizes) szoba kulcsát kérem** Ow (tee-zesh) sow-baw kool- chaat kay-rem
Please may I have ...	**Kaphatok kérem ...?** kop-hot-owk kay-rem ...?
a coat hanger?	**egy ruhaakasztót?** edj roohoh-okos-towt?
a towel?	**egy törölközőt?** edj töröl-közöt?

a glass? **egy poharat?**
edj pow-horot?

some soap? **szappant?**
sop-pont?

an ashtray? **egy hamutartót?**
edj homoo-tortowt?

another pillow? **még egy párnát?**
maig edj paar-naat?

another blanket? **még egy takarót?**
maig edj tokoh-rowt?

Come in! **Tessék!**
tesh-sheik!

One moment, please! **Egy pillanat!**
edj peel-lonot!

Please can you ... **Megtenné kérem, hogy ...**
megten-nay kay-rem, howdj ...

do this laundry? **kimosatja ezt?**
keemow-shot-yoh est?

have this dry-cleaned? **kitisztíttatja ezt?**
keetees-teet-totyoh est?

call me at ...? **feltelefonál nekem?**
fel-teleh-fownaal nekem?

help me with my luggage? **segít a csomagomat vinni?**
shegeet aw chow-mogow-mot
veen-nee?

call me a taxi for ...? **taxit hív nekem (6) órára?**
tok-seet heev nekem (hot)
owr-aa-roh?

[For times, see p. 123.]

The bill, please **Kérem a számlát**
kay-rem aw saam-laat

Is service included? **A felszolgálás benne van?**
aw felsowl-gaalaash ben-neh von?

I think this is wrong **Azt hiszem, itt tévedés van**
ozt hee-sem, eet tay-vedaish von

May I have a receipt? **Adjon kérem számlát**
od-yon kay-rem saam-laat

At breakfast

Some more ... please	**Kérek még egy kis ...** kay-rek maig edj keesh ...
coffee	**kávét** kaa-vait
tea	**teát** tey-aat
bread	**kenyeret** ken-yeh-ret
butter	**vajat** voy-ot
jam	**lekvárt** lek-vaart
May I have a boiled egg?	**Kaphatok egy lágytojást?** kop-hotok edj laadj-tow-yaasht?

LIKELY REACTIONS

Have you an identity document?	**Van igazolványa?** von eegoz-olvaan-yoh?
May I have your passport?	**Kérem az útlevelét** kay-rem oz ootleveh-lait
What's your name? *[see p. 16.]*	**Kérem a nevét** kay-rem aw neh-vait
Sorry, we are full	**Sajnos telt ház van** shoy-nosh telt haaz von
I haven't any rooms left	**Nincs szabad szobánk** ninch so-bod sow-baank
Do you want to have a look?	**Meg akarja nézni?** meg okor-yoh naiz-ny?
How many people is it for?	**Hány személyre?** haanj se-may-reh?
From (7 o'clock) onwards	**(Hét órá)tól** (hait ow-raa)towl
From (midday) onwards	**(Déli tizenkét órá)tól** (daily teezen-kait ow-raa)towl
[For times, see p. 123.] It's (100) forints	**(Száz) forintba kerül** (saaz) fow-reent-bow keh-rool

[For numbers, see p. 121.]

Camping and youth hostelling

ESSENTIAL INFORMATION

Camping

- Look for the word: **KEMPING**
- Be prepared for the following charges:
  per person
  for the car (if applicable)
  for the tent or caravan plot
  for electricity
  for hot showers
- You must provide proof of identity, such as your passport.
- It is forbidden to camp outside official camping sites.
- It is forbidden to camp in the lay-bys off the motorways.
- It is usually not possible to make advance reservations on camping sites. Try and secure a site in mid-afternoon if you are traveling during the high season.
- Owners of camping sites are not liable for losses. You should make your own insurance arrangements in advance.

Youth hostels

- Look for the words: **DIÁKSZÁLLÓ**
                       IFJÚSÁGI SZÁLLÓ
- There are but a few in Hungary; usually in larger cities, where during the summer season university dormitories are made use of as youth hostels or rather cheap accommodation for tourists.
- YHA card recommended.
- There is no upper age limit at Hungarian youth hostels.
- The charge for the night is the same for all ages, but some hostels are dearer than others.
- Accommodation is usually in small dormitories.
- Many Hungarian youth hostels do not provide a kitchen in which visitors can prepare their own meals; inexpensive food is though usually available either in the hostel or nearby.
- Finding a campsite and a youth hostel, *see p. 20*.
- Replacing equipment, *see p. 53*.

WHAT TO SAY

I have a booking	**Szobafoglalásom van**
	sow-boh-fowg-loh-laashom von
Have you any vacancies?	**Van szabad helyük?**
	Von sobod hey-ook?

It's for ...
one/two persons
egy/két személyre
edj/kait semay-reh

one/two adults
egy/két felnőtt számára
edj/kait felnöt saa-maa-roh

and one child
és egy gyerek számára
aish edj djerek saa-maa-roh

and two children
és két gyerek számára
aish kait djerek saa-maa-roh

It's for...
one week
egy hétre
edj hait-reh

two weeks
két hétre
kait hait-reh

How much is it...
Mennyit fizetek...
menjeet fee-zetek

for the tent?
a sátorért?
aw shaatowr-airt?

for the caravan?
a lakókocsiért?
aw lokow-kowchy-airt?

for the car?
az autóért?
oz oh-ootow-airt?

for the electricity?
az áramért?
oz aarom-airt?

per person?
személyenként?
semay-en-kaint?

per day?
naponként?
nopown-kaint?

per night?
éjszakánként?
ay-sokaan-kaint?

May I look around?
Körülnézhetek?
köröol-naiz-hetek?

At what time do you lock
up at night?
**Hánykor zárnak
esténként?**
haanj-kowr zaarnok eshtain-kaint?

Do you provide anything... **Lehet itt valamit ...**
lehet eet volumeet ...

  to eat? **enni?**
  en-nee?

  to drink? **inni?**
  een-nee?

Do you have ... **Van itt ...**
von eet ...

  a bar? **büfé?**
  boofay?

  hot showers? **meleg zuhany?**
  melegh zoohonj?

  a kitchen? **konyha?**
  konj-ho?

  a launderette? **mosoda?**
  mow-show-dow?

  a restaurant? **vendéglő?**
  ven-daig-lö?

  a shop? **vegyesbolt?**
  vedjesh-bolt?

  a swimming pool? **úszómedence?**
  oosow-medentse?

  a snack-bar? **büfé?**
  boofay?

[For food shopping, see p. 59. and for eating and drinking out see p. 76.]

Where are/is ... **Hol van ...**
hol von ...

  the dustbins? **a szemétláda?**
  ow semait-laa-doh?

  the showers? **a zuhanyozó?**
  ow zoohonj-ozow?

  the toilets? **a vécé?**
  aw vey-tsey?

  the fridge? **a hűtőszekrény?**
  aw hootow-sek-rainj?

Please, have you got ... **Kaphatok kérem...**
kop-hotok kairem ...

  a broom? **egy söprűt?**
  edj shöp-root?

  a corkscrew? **egy dugóhúzót?**
  edj doogow-hoozowt?

a drying-up cloth?	**egy konyharuhát?** edj konjhoh-roohaat?
a fork?	**egy villát?** edj vil-laat?
a frying pan?	**egy serpenyőt?** edj sher-penjöt?
an iron?	**egy vasalót?** edj voshoh-lowt?
a knife?	**egy kést?** edj kaisht?
a plate?	**egy tányért?** edj taa-njairt?
a saucepan?	**egy lábost?** edj laa-bosht?
a teaspoon?	**egy kávéskanalat?** edj kaavaish-konolot?
a tin opener?	**egy konzervnyitót?** edj konverv-njee-towt?
any washing powder?	**egy kis mosóport?** edj keesh moshow-powrt?
any washing-up liquid?	**egy kis mosogatószert?** edj keesh moshow-gotow-sert?
The bill, please	**Kérem a számlát** kairem aw saam-laat

Problems

The toilet	**a vécé** aw vey-tsey
The shower	**a zuhany** aw zoo-honj
The tap	**a csap** aw chop
The razor point	**a villanyborotva csatlakozója** aw vil-lonj-bow-rotvoh chotloh-kowzow-yoh
The light	**a villany** aw vil-lonj
... is not working	**... nem működik** ... nem mooködik
My camping gas has run out	**kifogyott a gázpalackom** keefow-djot aw gaaz-polots-kom

LIKELY REACTIONS

Have you an identity document/
  membership card/passport?

**Kérem az igazolványát/
útlevelét**
kairaem oz eegozowl-vaanjaat/
oot-leh-veh-lait

What's your name?
[See p. 16.]

Kérem a nevét
kairem aw neh-vait

Sorry, we are full

Sajnálom, nincs üres hely
shoy-naalom, ninch ooresh hey

How many people is it for?

Hány személyre?
haanj se-may-reh?

How many nights is it for?

Hány éjszakára?
haanj ay-sokaa-roh?

It's (100) forints ...

(Száz) forintba kerül ...
(saaz) fow-rint-bow kerool ...

  per day

naponta
nopontoh

  per night

éjszakánként
ay-sokaan-kaint

[For numbers, see p. 121.]

Rented accommodation: problem solving

ESSENTIAL INFORMATION

- If you are looking for accommodation to rent, look out for:
  SZOBA KIADÓ
  ZIMMER FREI (in German!)
  FIZETŐVENDÉGLÁTÓ
  VENDÉGSZOBA
- For arranging details of your let, *see* "Hotel" *p. 27*.
- Key words you are likely to meet if renting on the spot:
  Letét, előleg   deposit
  le-tait, eh-lö-leg
  Kulcs   key
  koolch
- Having arranged your own accommodation and arrived with the key, check the obvious basics that you take for granted at home.
  Electricity: Voltage? Razors and small appliances brought from home will probably need adjusting. You will also need an adaptor for the plugs.
  Gas: Town gas or bottled gas? Butane gas must be kept indoors, propane gas must be kept outdoors. In most cases however you will need propane-butane containers.
  Stove: Don't be surprised to find:
  — the grill inside the oven or no grill at all.
  — a lid covering the rings which lifts up to form a "splashback".
  Toilet: Main drainage or septic tank? Don't flush disposable diapers or anything else down the toilet whether on a septic tank or main drainage.
  Water: Find the stopcock. Check taps and plugs — they may not operate in the way you are used to. Check how to turn on (or light) the hot water.
  Windows: Check the method of opening and closing windows and shutters. At most places you will find venetian blinds instead of shutters.
  Insects: Usually not a problem except for mosquitos near beaches. Get an insecticide spray locally.
  Equipment: For buying or replacing equipment, *see p. 53*.
- You will probably have an official agent, but be clear in your own mind who to contact in an emergency, even if it is only a neighbor in the first place.

WHAT TO SAY

My name is ...	**(your name) vagyok**
	(your name) vodjok
I'm staying at ...	**(address) vagyok megszállva**
	(address) vodjok megsaal-voh
They've cut off ...	**Kikapcsolták ...**
	kikop-chowl-taak ...
the electricity	**a villanyt**
	aw vil-lonjt
the gas	**a gázt**
	aw gaazt
the water	**a vizet**
	aw vee-zet
Is there ... in the area?	**Van itt a környéken ...**
	von it aw kör-njaiken ...
an electrician	**villanyszerelő?**
	vil-lownj-serelö?
a plumber	**vízvezeték-szerelő?**
	veez-vezetaik-serelö?
a gas fitter	**gázszerelő?**
	gaaz-serelö?
Where is ...	**Hol van ...**
	hol von ...
the fuse box?	**a biztosíték?**
	aw beez-tow-sheetaik?
the stopcock?	**a főcsap?**
	aw fö-chop?
the boiler?	**a bojler?**
	aw boy-ler?
the water heater?	**a vízmelegítő?**
	aw veez-melegeetö?
Is there ...	**Mi van itt:**
	me von it:
town gas?	**városi gáz?**
	vaa-roshy gaaz?
bottled gas?	**palackos gáz?**
	polots-kosh gaaz?
a septic tank?	**emésztőgödör?**
	emaistö-gö-dör?
central heating?	**központi fűtés?**
	köz-ponty foo-taish?

The cooker	**a tűzhely** aw tooz-hey
The hair dryer	**a hajszárító** aw hoi-saa-reetow
The heating	**a fűtés** aw foo-taish
The boiler	**a bojler** aw boy-ler
The iron	**a vasaló** aw voshow-low
The pilot light	**az őrláng** oz ör-laang
The refrigerator	**a hűtőszekrény** aw hootö-sek-rainj
The telephone	**a telefon** aw teleh-fown
The toilet	**a vécé** aw vey-tsey
The washing machine	**a mosógép** aw moshow-gaip
The water heater	**a vízmelegítő** aw veez-melegee-tö
... is not working	**... nem működik** ... nem mookö-dik
Where can I get ...	**Hol kapok ...** hol ko-powk ...
an adaptor for this?	**egy adaptert ehhez?** edj oh-doptert eh-hez?
a bottle of butane gas?	**egy palack butángázt?** edj polots-kh bootaan-gaazt?
a bottle of propane gas?	**egy palack propángázt?** edj polots-kh propaan-gaazt?
a fuse?	**egy biztosítékot?** edj beez-toshee-taikot?
an insecticide spray	**egy rovarölő sprayt?** edj row-vor-ölö sprait?
a light bulb?	**egy villanykörtét?** edj vil-lonj-körtait?
The drain	**a lefolyó** aw lefow-yow
The sink	**a mosogató** aw moshow-gatow

The toilet	**a vécé** aw vey-tsey
... is blocked	**... el van dugulva** ... el von doogool-voh
The gas is leaking	**Szivárog a gáz** see-vaa-rog aw gaaz
Can you mend it straightaway?	**Meg tudja javítani azonnal?** meg toodyow yo-veetony ozown-nol?
When can you mend it?	**Mikor tudja megjavítani?** meekor toodjow meg-yow-veetony?
How much do I owe you?	**Mennyivel tartozom?** men-yeevel tor-tozom?
When is the rubbish collected?	**Mikor viszik el a szemetet?** meekor vee-sik el aw semetet?

LIKELY REACTIONS

What's your name?	**Mi a neve?** mee aw neh-veh?
What's your address?	**Mi a címe?** mee aw tsee-meh?
There is a shop ...	**Van egy bolt ...** von edj bowlt ...
in town	**a városban** aw vaa-roshbon
in the village	**a faluban** aw fo-loobon
I can't come ...	**Nem tudok eljönni ...** nem toodok el-yön-ny
today	**ma** mah
this week	**ezen a héten** ezen aw haiten
I can't come until Monday	**Csak hétfön tudok eljönni** chok haitfoon toodok el-yown-ny
I can come ...	**El tudok jönni ...** el toodok yown-ny
on Tuesday	**kedden** ked-den
when you want	**amikor akarja** omee-kor okor-yoh

Every day	**Mindennap**
	meenden-nop
Every other day	**Minden másnap**
	meenden maash-nop
On Wednesdays	**Minden szerdán**
	meenden ser-daan

[For days of the week, p. 125.]

General shopping

The drugstore / The chemist's

ESSENTIAL INFORMATION

- There are two kinds of drugstore in Hungary. The **GYÓGY-SZERTÁR** (dispensing chemist's) is the place to go for prescriptions, medicines, etc., while toilet and household articles are sold at the **HÁZTARTÁSI BOLT** (chemist's shop).
- Look for the words:
  GYÓGYSZERTÁR
  PATIKA
  or:
  HÁZTARTÁSI BOLT
  ILLATSZER (this will be the sign also at department stores)
  Try the **GYÓGYSZERTÁR** *before* going to a doctor: they are usually qualified to treat minor injuries or ailments.
- The **GYÓGYSZERTÁR** is open during normal business hours and take it in turn to stay open all night and on Sundays. If the nearest is shut, a notice on the door will give the address of the nearest night and Sunday service: **ÜGYELETES GYÓGY-SZERTÁR.**
- Finding a drugstore, *see p. 20*.

WHAT TO SAY

I'd like ...	**Kérek...**
	kai-rek ...
some antiseptic	**valami fertőtlenítőt**
	volomy fertöt-le-neetöt
some aspirin	**aszpirint**
	os-pireent
some bandages	**kötszert**
	köt-sert
some cotton wool	**vattát**
	vot-taat
some eye drops	**szemcseppet**
	sem-chep-pet

some foot powder	**lábhintőport** laab-hintö-powrt
some gauze dressing	**mullpólyát** mull-pow-yaat
some inhalant	**kamillát** komil-laat
some insect repellent	**rovarirtót** rovor-eer-towt
some lip salve	**ajakírt** oyok-eert
some nose drops	**orrcseppet** orr-chep-pet
some sticking plaster	**ragtapaszt** rog-topost
some throat pastilles	**torokpasztillát** torok-pos-teel-laat
some Vaseline	**vazelint** vo-zeleent
I'd like something for ...	**Kérek valamit ...** kairek volomeet ...
bites (snakes, dogs)	**(kígyó, kutya) harapásra** (keedjow, kootjoh) horo- paash-roh
burns	**égésre** aigaish-reh
a cold	**hűlésre** hoolaish-reh
constipation	**székrekedésre** seik-rekedaish-reh
a cough	**köhögésre** kö-hö-gaish-reh
diarrhoea	**hasmenésre** hosh-menaish-reh
earache	**fülfájásra** fool-faa-yaash-roh
flu	**influenzára** in-floo-en-zaa-roh
scalds	**égésre** aigaish-reh
sore gums	**fájós fogínyre** faa-yowsh fog-eenj-reh
a sprain	**ficamra** fee-tsom-roh

stings (mosquitos, bees)	**(szúnyog, méh)csípésre** (soon-yog, maikh) cheepaish-reh
sunburn	**leégésre** leh-aigaish-reh
car/air/sea sickness	**tengeri betegségre** tengeree beteg-shaig-reh
I need ...	**Kellene nekem ...** kel-le-neh ne-kem ...
some baby food	**valami bébiétel** volomy bai-bee-aitel
some contraceptives	**néhány óvszer** nai-haanj owv-ser
some deodorant	**valami dezodor** volomy dez-odowr
some disposable nappies	**egy csomag eldobható pelenka** edj chow-mogh el-dob-hotow pelen-kah
some handcream	**valami kézkrém** volomy kaiz-kraim
some lipstick	**egy rúzs** edj roozh
some make-up remover	**egy üveg arclemosó** edj oovegh orts-le-moshow
some paper tissues	**egy csomag papírzsebkendő** edj chow-mogh popeer-zheb- ken-dö
some razor blades	**egy csomag borotvapenge** edj chow-mogh borotvoh-pen-ghe
some safety pins	**néhány biztosítótű** nai-honj beezt-sheeoh too
some sanitary towels	**egy csomag egészségügyi betét** edj chow-mogh egais-shaig- oodjee be-tait
some shaving cream	**valami borotvakrém** volomy borotvoh-kraim
some soap	**egy darab szappan** edj dorob sop-pon
some suntan lotion/oil	**valami naptej/olaj** volomy nop-tey/owloy
some talcum powder	**egy doboz púder** edj doboz pooder
some Tampax	**egy csomag tampon** edj chow-mogh tahm-pon

some toilet paper	**egy csomag vécépapír**
	edj chow-mogh vaitsai-popeer
some toothpaste	**egy tubus fogkrém**
	edj toobush fog-kraim

[For other essential expressions, see "Shop talk", p. 56.]

Holiday items

ESSENTIAL INFORMATION

- Places to shop at and signs to look for:
  ÁPISZ (stationery)
  OFOTÉRT (films)
  IPARMŰVÉSZET (arts and crafts)
  AJÁNDÉK (gifts)
- The main department store chains:
  CENTRUM
  SKÁLA

WHAT TO SAY

Where can I buy ...?	**Hol kapok ...?**
	hol koh-pok ...?
I'd like ...	**Szeretnék venni ...**
	seretnaik ven-ny ...
a bag	**egy táskát**
	edj taash-kaat
a beach ball	**egy strandlabdát**
	edj shtrond-lob-daat
a bucket	**egy vödröt**
	edj vöd-röt
an English newspaper	**egy angol újságot**
	edj on-gowl ooy-shaagowt
some envelopes	**néhány borítékot**
	nai-honj boree-taikot
a guidebook	**egy útikönyvet**
	edj ooty-konj-vet

a map (of the area)	**egy térképet (a környékről)**
	edj tair-kaipet (aw kör-njaik-röl)
some postcards	**néhány képeslapot**
	nai-honj kaipesh-lo-pot
a spade	**egy ásót**
	edj aah-showt
a straw hat	**egy szalmakalapot**
	edj solmoh-kolopot
a suitcase	**egy bőröndöt**
	edj bö-rön-döt
some sunglasses	**egy napszemüveget**
	edj nop-semooh-veghet
a sunshade	**egy napernyőt**
	edj nop-er-njöt
an umbrella	**egy esernyőt**
	edj esher-njöt
some writing paper	**géppapírt**
	gaip-poh-peert
a color film	**egy színes filmet**
	edj seenesh filmet
for prints	**papírképhez**
	popeer-kaiphez
for slides	**diafilmhez**
	dee-aw-filmhez
a black and white film	**egy fekete-fehér filmet**
	edj fekete-fehair filmet
a super 8 film	**egy szuper nyolcas filmet**
	edj sooper njol-tsosh filmet
some flash bulbs	**néhány vaku lámpát**
	nai-honj vah-koo laam-paat
This camera is broken	**Elromlott a fényképezőgépem**
	el-rom-lot aw fainj-kaip-ezöh-gaipem
The film is stuck	**Megakadt benne a film**
	meg-okot ben-neh aw film
Please can you ...	**Legyen szíves ...**
	ledjen seevesh ...
develop this?	**előhívni ezt**
	elö-heev-ny est
print this?	**képeket csinálni erről**
	kaipeket cheenaal-ny er-röl
load the camera?	**betölteni a filmet**
	be-töl-teny aw filmet

The smoke shop

ESSENTIAL INFORMATION

- A smoke shop is called:
  TRAFIK
  DOHÁNYBOLT
- Large supermarkets and department stores often have their own "smoke shop" on the premises, a kind of stall near the entrance or cash registers.
- The smoke shop is the only place where you can get tobacco, cigars, pipe utensils, flints etc., whereas cigarettes can be bought at a variety of places:
  at the **KIOSZK** (a hut in the street)
  at most foodstores
  inside a café, bar, pub, etc.
- To ask if there is a smoke shop near by, *see p. 20*.

WHAT TO SAY

A packet of cigarettes ...	**Egy csomag ... cigarettát** edj chomawg ... tsee-goh-ret-taat
with filters	**filteres** filteresh
without filters	**filter nélküli** filter nail-kooly
king size	**extra hosszú** ekstroh hos-sooh
menthol	**mentolos** men-towl-osh
Those up there...	**Azt kérem ...** ost kairem ...
on the right	**jobbra** yob-rah
on the left	**balra** bol-rah
Those up there [point]	**Azt, ott fönn** ost, owt fönn
Cigarettes, please	**Cigarettát kérek** tsee-goh-ret-taat kairek

100, 200, 300	**száz, kétszáz, háromszáz** saaz, kait-saaz, haarom-saaz
Two packets	**két doboz** kait do-boz

Have you got ...   **Van itt ...**
von eet ...

   English cigarettes?   **angol cigaretta?**
on-gowl tsee-gaw-ret-toh?

   American cigarettes?   **amerikai cigaretta?**
omeree-kow-ee tsee-gaw-ret-toh?

   English pipe tobacco?   **angol pipadohány?**
on-gowl peepoh-dow-haanj?

   American pipe tobacco?   **amerikai pipadohány?**
omeree-kow-ee peepoh-dow-haanj?

   rolling tobacco?   **cigaretta dohány?**
tsee-gaw-ret-toh dow-haanj?

I'd like ...   **Kérek ...**
kairek ...

   a packet of pipe tobacco   **egy csomag pipadohányt**
edj chow-mog peepoh-dow-haanjt

   some cigars, please   **szivart**
see-vowrt

   a box of matches   **egy doboz gyufát**
edj dow-boz djoofaat

   a packet of pipe cleaners   **egy csomag pipatisztítót**
edj chow-mog pee-poh-tis-teetowt

   a packet of flints   **egy csomag tűzkövet**
edj chow-mog toos-kö-vet

   lighter fuel   **öngyújtóhoz benzint**
ön-djooy-tow-hos ben-zeent

   lighter gas   **öngyújtóhoz gázt**
ön-djooy-tow-hos gaast

That one down there ...   **Azt, ott lenn**
ost, owt lenn

   on the right   **jobbra**
yob-roh

   on the left   **balra**
bol-roh

This one [point]   **Ezt kérem**
est kairem

Those [point]   **Azt kérem**
ost kairem

[For other essential expressions, see "Shop talk", p. 56.]

Buying clothes

ESSENTIAL INFORMATION

- Look for:
  RUHÁZATI BOLT (clothes)
  CIPŐBOLT (shoes)
- Don't buy without being measured first or without trying things on.
- Don't rely on conversion charts of clothing sizes [see p. 136].
- If you are buying for someone else, take their measurements with you.
- All major department stores [see p. 45.] sell clothes and shoes.

WHAT TO SAY

I'd like ...	Szeretnék ...
	seretnaik ...
an anorak	**egy anorákot**
	edj on-ow-raak-ot
a belt	**egy övet**
	edj övet
a bikini	**egy bikinit**
	edj bikinit
a bra	**egy melltartót**
	edj mell-tor-towt
a cap (swimming)	**egy úszósapkát**
	edj oosow-shop-kaat
(skiing)	**egy sísapkát**
	edj shee-shop-kaat
a cardigan	**egy kardigánt**
	edj kor-dee-gaant
a coat	**egy kabátot**
	edj ko-baatowt
a dress	**egy ruhát**
	edj roo-haat
a hat	**egy kalapot**
	edj kolopot
a jacket	**egy dzsekit**
	edj dzhekeet

a jumper	**egy pulóvert** edj pool-ow-vert
a nightdress	**egy hálóinget** edj haalow-een-ghet
some pyjamas	**egy pizsamát** edj pizhow-maat
a raincoat	**egy esőkabátot** edj eshö-koh-baatowt
a shirt (women)	**egy blúzt** edj bloozt
a shirt (men)	**egy inget** edj een-ghet
a skirt	**egy szoknyát** edj soknjaat
a swimsuit	**egy fürdőruhát** edj foordö-roohaat
some tights	**egy harisnyanadrágot** edj horish-njoh-nodraagot
some trousers	**egy nadrágot** edj nodraagot
a T-shirt	**egy pólót** edj poh-loht
I'd like a pair of ...	**Szeretnék egy ...** seretnaik edj ...
briefs (women)	**egy bugyit** edj boodjeet
gloves	**egy kesztyűt** edj kestjoot
jeans	**egy farmert** edj formert
shorts	**egy rövidnadrágot** edj rö-veed-nod-raagot
(short/long) socks	**egy (boka/térd)zoknit** edj (boka/taird)zok-neet
stockings	**egy harisnyát** edj horish-njaat
underpants (men)	**egy alsónadrágot** edj olshow-nod-raagot
I'd like a pair of ...	**Szeretnék egy pár ...** seretnaik edj paar ...
shoes	**cipőt** tsee-pöt
canvas shoes	**vászoncipőt** vaason-tsee-pöt

sandals	**szandált** son-daalt
beach shoes	**strandcipőt** shtrond-tsee-pöt
smart shoes	**esti cipőt** eshty tsee-pöt
moccasins	**mokaszint** mokoh-seent
My size is ...	**Az én méretem ...** oz ain mairetem ...

[For numbers, see p. 121.]

Can you measure me, please?	**Megmérné a méretemet?** megmair-ney aw mairetemet?
Can I try it on?	**Felpróbálhatom?** felprow-baal-hotom?
It's for a present	**Ajándék lesz** oyaan-daik les
These are the measurements *[show written]*	**Ez az illető mérete** ez oz eel-lető maireteh
bust	**mellbőség** mel-bö-shaig
chest	**mellbőség** mel-bö-shaig
collar	**nyakbőség** njok-bö-shaig
hip	**csípőszélesség** cheepö-sailesh-shaig
leg	**nadrágszár** nodraag-saar
waist	**derékbőség** deraik-bö-shaig
Have you got something ...	**Tudna valamit mutatni ...** toodnoh volomeet moototny ...
in black?	**feketében?** feketai-ben?
in white?	**fehérben?** fehair-ben?
in gray?	**szürkében?** soorkey-ben?
in blue?	**kékben?** kaik-ben?
in brown?	**barnában?** bornaa-bon?

in pink?	**rózsaszínben?**
	rowzhoh-seen-ben?
in green?	**zöldben?**
	zöld-ben?
in red?	**pirosban?**
	peerosh-bon?
in yellow?	**sárgában?**
	shaar-gaa-bon?
in this color?	**ebben a színben?**
	[point] eb-ben aw seen-ben?
in cotton?	**vászonban?**
	vaa-son-bon?
in denim?	**farmerben?**
	former-ben?
in leather?	**bőrben?**
	bör-ben?
in nylon?	**nejlonban?**
	naay-lon-bon?
in suede?	**antilopban?**
	ontee-lop-bon?
in wool?	**gyapjúban?**
	djop-yoo-bon?
in this material? [point]	**ebben az anyagban?**
	eb-ben oz onjog-bon?

[For other essential expressions, see "Shop talk", p. 56.]

Replacing equipment

ESSENTIAL INFORMATION

- Look for these shops and signs:
  VASEDÉNY (hardware)
  HÁZTARTÁSI BOLT (household goods)
  ELEKTROMOS CIKKEK (electrical goods)
- In a supermarket, look for this display:
  HÁZTARTÁSI CIKKEK
- To ask the way to the shop, *see p. 20.*
- At a campsite try their shop first.

WHAT TO SAY

Have you got ...	**Kaphatnék ...** kophot-naik ...
an adaptor? *[show appliance]*	**egy adaptert?** edj odop-tert?
a bottle of butane gas?	**egy palack butángázt?** edj polots-kh bootaan-gaazt?
a bottle of propane gas?	**egy palack propángázt?** edj polots-kh prow-paan-gaazt?
a bottle opener?	**egy sörnyitót?** edj shör-njee-towt?
a corkscrew?	**egy dugóhúzót?** edj doogow-hoozowt?
any disinfectant?	**valami fertőtlenítőszert?** volomy fertöt-leny-tö-sert?
any disposable cups?	**néhány papírpoharat?** nei-honj poh-peer-pow-ho-rot?
any disposable plates?	**néhány papírtányért?** nei-honj poh-peer-taah-njairt?
a drying-up cloth?	**egy törlőruhát?** edj tör-lö-roohaat?
any forks?	**egy villát?** edj veel-laat?
a fuse *[show old one]*	**egy biztosítékot?** edj beeztow-shee-taikot?
an insecticide spray?	**egy rovarölő sprayt?** edj rovor-ölö sprayt?

a paper kitchen roll?	**egy tekercs törlőpapírt?**
	edj tekerch tör-löh-poh-peert?
any knives?	**egy kést?**
	edj kaisht?
a light bulb [show]	**egy villanykörtét?**
	old one]edj vil-lonj-kör-tait?
a plastic bucket?	**egy műanyag vödröt?**
	edj moo-onjogh vöd-röt?
a plastic can?	**egy műanyag kannát?**
	edj moo-onjogh kon-naat?
a scouring pad?	**egy dörzspárnát?**
	edj dörzh-paar-naat?
a spanner?	**egy csavarkulcsot?**
	edj chovor-kool-chot?
a sponge?	**egy szivacsot?**
	edj see-votchot?
any string?	**egy zsineget?**
	edj zhee-neget?
any tent pegs?	**egy sátorcölöpöt**
	edj shaator-tsöh-löh-pöt?
a tin opener?	**egy konzervnyitót?**
	edj konzerv-njeetowt?
a torch?	**egy elemlámpát?**
	edj elem-laam-paat?
any torch batteries?	**zseblámpaelemet?**
	zheb-laampoh-elemet?
a universal plug (for the sink)?	**egy lefolyó dugót?**
	edj leh-foyow doogowt?
a washing line?	**egy ruhaszárító kötelet?**
	edj roohow-saareetow kö-telet?
any washing powder?	**valami mosóport?**
	volomy moh-show-port?
a washing-up brush?	**egy mosogatókefét?**
	edj moshow-gotow-kefait?
any washing-up liquid?	**valami mosogatószert?**
	volomy moshow-gotow-sert?

[For other essential expressions, see "Shop talk", p. 56.]

Shop talk

ESSENTIAL INFORMATION

- Know your coins and bills.
  Hungarian coins: 0.10; 0.20; 0.50 fillér [fil-lair] 1.00; 2.00;
  5.00; 10.00; 20.00 **Forint** [fowrint]
  see illustration
  Hungarian notes: 10; 20; 50; 100; 500; 1000; 5000 Forint
- Know how to say the important weights and measures. It is not
  usual to use grams; Hungarians use **deka** (=1 dekagram: 10
  grams) instead.

50 grams	**öt (5) deka** öt dey-kah
100 grams	**tíz (10) deka** teez dey-kah
200 grams	**húsz (20) deka** hoos dey-kah
1 kilo	**egy (1) kiló** edj kee-low
2 kilos	**két (2) kiló** keit kee-low
1/2 liter	**fél (1/2) liter** fail lee-ter
1 liter	**egy (1) liter** edj lee-ter
2 liters	**két (2) liter** keit lee-ter

[For numbers, see p. 121.]

- In small shops don't be surprised if customers, as well as the
  shop assistant, say "hello" and "good-bye" to you.

CUSTOMER

Hello	**Jó napot (kívánok)** jow-nopot (kee-vaa-nok)
Good morning	**Jó reggelt (kívánok)** yow-reg-gelt (kee-vaa-nok)
Good afternoon	**Jó napot (kívánok)** yow-nopot (kee-vaa-nok)

Good-bye	**Viszontlátásra**
	veesont-laa-taash-roh
I'm just looking	**Csak nézegetek**
	chok naizeh-ghetek
Excuse me	**Bocsánat**
	bochaa-not
How much is this/that?	**Mibe kerül ez/az?**
	meebeh kerool es/os?
I'd like that, please	**Azt kérem**
	ost kairem
Not that	**Azt nem kérem**
	ost nem kairem
That's enough, thank you	**Köszönöm, ennyi elég**
	kö-sö-nöm, enjee elaig
More, please	**Még kérek**
	maig kairek
Less than that	**Ennél kevesebbet kérek**
	en-nail kevesheb-bet kairek
That's fine	**Ez pont jó lesz**
	es pont yow less
I won't take it, thank you	**Köszönöm, de nem kérem**
	kö-sö-nöm, deh nem kairem
It's not right	**Nem lesz jó**
	nem less yow
Thank you very much	**Köszönöm szépen**
	kö-sö-nöm saipen
Have you got something...	**Nincs valami ...**
	ninch volomy ...
better?	**jobb?**
	yowb?
cheaper?	**olcsóbb?**
	ol-chowb?
different?	**más?**
	maash?
larger?	**nagyobb?**
	nodj-owb?
smaller?	**kisebb?**
	kee-sheb?
At what time do you ...	**Hánykor ...**
	honj-kor ...
open?	**nyitnak?**
	njeet-nok?
close?	**zárnak?**
	zaar-nok?

Can I have a bag, please? **Kaphatnék egy táskát?**
kophot-naik edj taash-kaat?

Can I have a receipt? **Kaphatnék egy számlát?**
kophot-naik edj saam-laat?

Do you take ...? **Elfogadnak ...**
elfogod-nok ...

   English/American money? **angol/amerikai pénzt is?**
on-gowl/omeree-koh-ee painzt ish?

   traveler's checks? **úticsekket is?**
ooty-chek-ket ish?

   credit cards? **hitelkártyát is?**
heetel-kor-tjaat ish?

I'd like ... **Kérek ...**
kairek ...

   one like that **egy ilyet**
edj ee-yet

   two like that **két ilyet**
keit ee-yet

SHOP ASSISTANT

Can I help you? **Mivel szolgálhatok?**
meevel solgaal-hotok?

What would you like? **Tessék parancsolni**
tesh-shaik poronchol-ny

Is that all? **Ez minden?**
es meen-den?

Anything else? **Valami egyebet?**
volomy edjeh-bet?

Would you like it wrapped? **Becsomagoljam?**
beh-chomogol-yom?

Sorry, none left **Sajnos, elfogyott**
shoy-nosh el-fow-djott

I haven't got any **Sajnos, nincsen**
shoy-nosh, neen-chen

I haven't got any left **Sajnos, nincs több**
shoy-nosh, ninch töb

How many do you want? **Mennyit parancsol?**
menj-njeet poron-chol?

Is that enough? **Ennyi elég lesz?**
enj-njee elaig less?

Shopping for food

Bread

ESSENTIAL INFORMATION

- Finding a baker's, *see p. 20*.
- Key words to look for:
  PÉK (baker)
  PÉKSÉG (baker's)
  KENYÉR (bread)
- Supermarkets of any size and general stores nearly always sell bread.
- Though many bakeries are famous for their special bread Hungarians usually buy their bread in supermarkets or general stores. Many bakers will close early afternoon even on weekdays.

WHAT TO SAY

Some bread, please	**Kenyeret kérek** kenjeh-ret kairek
A loaf (like that)	**Egy (ilyen) kenyeret kérek** edj (ee-yen) kenjeh-ret kairek
A large one	**Egy nagy kenyeret kérek** edj nodj kenjeh-ret kairek
A small one	**Egy kis kenyeret kérek** edj kish kenjeh-ret kairek
A bread roll	**Zsömle** zhömleh
A crescent roll	**Kifli** keefly
Bread	**Kenyér** kenj-air
Sliced bread	**Szeletelt kenyér** seletelt kenj-air
White bread	**Fehér kenyér** fehair kenj-air
Rye bread	**Rozskenyér** rozh-kenj-air

(Black) rye bread	**Fekete kenyér**
	fekete kenj-air
Two loaves	**Két kenyér**
	kait kenj-air
Four bread rolls	**Négy zsömle**
	naidj zhömleh
Four crescent rolls	**Négy kifli**
	naidj keflee

[For other essential expressions, see "Shop talk", p. 56.]

Cakes

ESSENTIAL INFORMATION

- Key words to look for:
  CUKRÁSZDA (cake shop, often with a few tables to seat customers)
  ESZPRESSZÓ (coffee-shop — a place to buy cakes and have a drink at a table, though not wine; *see also p. 76*. "Ordering a drink")

WHAT TO SAY

The types of cakes you find in the shops vary slightly but the following are some of the most common:

Dobostorta	a chocolate tart with glazed caramel top
Sacher-torta	rich chocolate cake with jam
Rigó Jancsi	whipped chocolate cake with chocolate topping
Rétes	flaky pastry filled with apple, nuts and raisins or poppy seeds
Krémes	flake pastry filled with rich cream
Gyümölcs-torta	fruit on a sponge base with glazing over or cream
Túrós	cheesecake
Minyon	small portions of almost any of the above glazed over

You usually buy individual pastries by number:

Two rétes (strudel), please   **Két rétest kérek**
kait raitesht kairek

You buy large cakes by the slice:
One slice of fruit tart   **Egy szelet gyümölcstorta**
edj selet djoo-mölch-towr-tah
Two slices of Dobos-tart   **Két szelet Dobostorta**
kait selet Dowbosh-towr-tah
[For other essential expressions, see "Shop talk", p. 56.]

Ice-cream and sweets

ESSENTIAL INFORMATION

- Key words to look for:
  FAGYLALT or **FAGYI** (ice-cream)
  FAGYLALTOZÓ (ice-cream parlour)
  ÉDESSÉGBOLT (sweet-shop)
- Prepacked sweets and biscuits are available in general stores and supermarkets.

WHAT TO SAY

A ... ice, please	**Egy ... fagylaltot kérek**
	edj ... fodj-loltowt kairek
strawberry	**eper**
	eh-pehr
chocolate	**csokoládé**
	chowkoh-laah-day
vanilla	**vanília**
	voneelee-oh
lemon	**citrom**
	tseet-rom
caramel	**karamella**
	korom-el-loh

At the table

A single portion	**Egy kisadag**
	edj kish-odog
Two single portions	**Két kisadag**
	kait kish-odog
A double portion	**Egy nagyadag**
	edj nodj-odog
Two double portions	**Két nagyadag**
	kait nodj-odog
A mixed ice ...	**Egy vegyes adag ...**
	edj vedj-esh odog
with whipped cream	**tejszínhabbal**
	tey-seen-hob-bol
without whipped cream	**hab nélkül**
	hob nail-kool

Over the counter

A cone ...	**Egy tölcsér ...**
	edj töl-chair ...
A tub ...	**Egy kehely ...**
	edj ke-hey ...
with two scoops	**két gombóccal**
	kait gom-bowts-tsol
with three scoops	**három gombóccal**
	haa-rom gom-bowts-tsol
(10 forint) worth of ice-cream	**(Tíz forintért) kérek fagylaltot**
	(Tees fowrin-tairt) kairek fodj-lowl-tot
A packet of ...	**Egy zacskó ...**
	edj zoch-kow ...
100 grams of ...	**(10) deka ...**
	(Tees) dey-koh ...
200 grams of ...	**(20) deka ...**
	(Hoos) dey-koh ...
sweets	**cukorka**
	tsookowr-koh
toffees	**karamellás cukorka**
	koromel-laash tsookowr-koh
chocolates	**praliné**
	prow-lee-nay
mints	**mentolos cukorka**
	mentowlosh tsookowr-koh
A lollipop	**egy nyalóka**
	edj njolow-koh

[For other essential expressions, see "Shop talk", p. 56.]

In the supermarket

ESSENTIAL INFORMATION

- The place to ask for: *[see p. 20.]*
  ABC ÁRUHÁZ
  KÖZÉRT (general food store)
- Key instructions on signs in the shop:
  BEJÁRAT (entrance)
  KIJÁRAT (exit)
  PÉNZTÁR (checkout, cash desk)
- Large supermarkets are open all day from 8.00 a.m. to 6.30, 7.00 or 8.00 in the evening. In larger cities there are plenty of shops open all night, the selection however is usually limited.
- For nonfood items, *see* "Replacing equipment", *p. 53*.
- No need to say anything in a supermarket, but ask if you can't see what you want.

WHAT TO SAY

Excuse me, please ...	**Bocsánat ...**
	bow-chaanot ...
Where is ...	**Hol van ...**
	Howl von ...
the bread?	**a kenyér?**
	aw kenj-air?
the butter?	**a vaj?**
	aw voy?
the cheese?	**a sajt?**
	aw shoyt?
the chocolate?	**a csokoládé?**
	aw chow-kowlaa-day?
the coffee?	**a kávé?**
	aw kah-vay?
the cooking oil?	**az étolaj?**
	os ait-owloy?
the meat?	**a tőkehús?**
	aw tö-keh-hoosh?
the fruit?	**a gyümölcs?**
	aw djoo-mölch?

the jam?	**a lekvár?**
	aw lek-vaar?
the milk?	**a tej?**
	aw tey?
the mineral water?	**az ásványvíz?**
	oz aash-vaanj veez?
the salt?	**a só?**
	aw show?
the sugar?	**a cukor?**
	aw tsoo-kor?
the tea?	**a tea?**
	aw tey-oh?
the vegetable section?	**a zöldségosztály?**
	aw zöld-shaig-ows-taay?
the vinegar?	**az ecet?**
	os eh-tset?
the wine?	**a bor?**
	aw bowr?
the beer?	**a sör?**
	aw shör?
the yoghurt?	**a joghurt?**
	aw yog-hoort?
Where are ...	**Hol van ...**
	hol von ...
the biscuits?	**a keksz?**
	aw keks?
the crisps?	**a burgonyaszirom?**
	aw boor-ghownjoh-see-rom?
the eggs?	**a tojás?**
	aw tow-yaash?
the frozen foods?	**a mélyhűtő?**
	aw mey-hoo-tö?
the fruit juices?	**a gyümölcslé?**
	aw djoo-mölch-ley?
the pastas?	**a tészta?**
	aw tey-stoh?
the soft drinks?	**az üdítőital?**
	os oodee-tö eetol?
the sweets?	**az édesség?**
	as aidesh-shaig?
the canned foods?	**a konzerv?**
	aw kown-zerv?

[For other essential expressions, see "Shop talk", p. 56.]

Picnic food

ESSENTIAL INFORMATION

- Key words to look for:
  CSEMEGE (delicatessen)
  HENTES or
  HÚSBOLT (butcher's)

WHAT TO SAY

One slice of ...	**Egy szelet ...**
	edj selet ...
Two slices of ...	**Két szelet ...**
	kait selet ...
roast beef	**sült bélszín**
	shoolt bail-seen
raw cured ham	**füstölt sonka**
	fooshtölt shon-koh
cooked ham	**gépsonka**
	gaip-shon-koh
garlic sausage	**kolbász**
	kol-baas
salami	**szalámi**
	saw-laa-mee
100 grams of ...	**Tíz (10) deka ...**
	tees (10) dey-koh ...
150 grams of ...	**Tizenöt (15) deka ...**
	teezen-öt (15) dey-koh ...
200 grams of ...	**Húsz (20) deka ...**
	hoos (20) dey-koh ...
300 grams of ...	**Harminc (30) deka ...**
	Hor-mints (30) dey-koh ...
herring salad	**halsaláta**
	hol-shawlaa-toh
egg and mayonnaise salad	**tojássaláta**
	toyaash shaw-laa-toh
chicken salad	**csirkesaláta**
	cheer-keh shaw-laa-toh
tomato salad	**paradicsomsaláta**
	poroh-deechom shaw-laa-toh

potato salad   **krumplisaláta**
                    kroomply-shaw-laa-toh

You might also like to try some of these:

lángos   a kind of pancake fried in oil
laan-gosh
libamáj   goose liver (fried or paté)
leeboh-maay
virsli   frankfurter sausages
virsh-lee
parasztkolbász   spicy, paprika-garlic sausage
pohrost-kol-baas
gombasaláta   mushroom salad
gom-boh shoh-laa-toh
pálpusztai   soft cheese
paal-poostoh-yee
parenyica   smoked cheese
porey-njee-tsoh
ementáli   Swiss cheese
eh-mentaah-ly
eidámi   Dutch cheese
ey-daah-mee
camembert/brie   camembert/brie
komom-ber/bree

[For other essential expressions, see "Shop talk", p. 56.]

Fruit and vegetables

ESSENTIAL INFORMATION

- Key words to look for:
  GYÜMÖLCS (fruit)
  ZÖLDSÉG (vegetables)
  ZÖLDSÉGES (greengrocer's)
- If possible, buy fruit and vegetables in the market where they are cheaper and fresher than in the shops.
- Weight guide:
  1 kilo of potatoes is sufficient for six people for one meal.

WHAT TO SAY

1 lb (1/2 kilo) of ...	**Fél (1/2) kiló ...**
	fail kee-low ...
1 kilo of ...	**Egy kiló ...**
	edj kee-low ...
2 kilos of ...	**Két kiló ...**
	kait kee-low ...
apricots	**sárgabarack**
	shaar-goh-boh-rots-kh
apples	**alma**
	ol-moh
bananas	**banán**
	boh-naan
cherries	**cseresznye**
	cheres-njeh
grapes	**szőlő**
	söh-löh
oranges	**narancs**
	noh-ronch
pears	**körte**
	kör-teh
peaches	**őszibarack**
	ösee-boh-rots-kh
plums	**szilva**
	seel-voh
strawberries	**eper**
	eh-perr

A water-melon, please	**Egy dinnyét kérek**
	edj dee-njait kairek
A melon	**egy sárgadinnye**
	edj shaar-goh-dee-njeh
A grapefruit	**egy grapefruit**
	edj graip-froot
1 lb of ...	**Fél (1/2) kiló ...**
	fail kee-low ...
1 kilo of ...	**Egy (1) kiló ...**
	edj kee-low ...
3 lbs of ...	**Másfél (1.5) kiló ...**
	maash-fail kee-low ...
2 kilo of ...	**Két (2) kiló ...**
	kait kee-low ...
carrots	**sárgarépa**
	shaar-go-raipah
green beans	**zöldbab**
	zöld-bob
leeks	**póréhagyma**
	powray-hodj-moh
mushrooms	**gomba**
	gowm-boh
onions	**hagyma**
	hodj-moh
peppers (green or white)	**zöldpaprika**
	zöld-popree-koh
peas	**borsó**
	bowr-show
potatoes	**burgonya**
	boorgh-ownj-oh
red cabbage	**vörös káposzta**
	vörösh kaa-pos-toh
spinach	**spenót**
	shpeh-nowt
tomatoes	**paradicsom**
	poro-dee-chom
A bunch of ...	**Egy csomag ...**
	edj csow-mog ...
parsley	**petrezselyem**
	petreh-zheyem
radishes	**retek**
	reh-tek
spring onions	**zöldhagyma**
	zöld-hodj-moh

Here are some fruit and vegetables which may not be familiar:

ringló ring-low	a kind of plum
meggy medj	sour-tasting variety of cherry
mandarin mondoreen	tangerine
karalábé koroh-laah-bay	vegetable similar to turnip
tök tök	pumpkin, prepared in a great variety of ways

[For other essential expressions, see "Shop talk", p. 56.]

beef/marha

1. nyak
2. tarja
3. hátszín
4. rostélyos
5. fartő
6. uszály
7. vastag szegy
8. lapocka
9. oldalas
10. hátsó comb
11. csontos szegy
12. puha szegy
13. lábszár

veal/borjú

1. nyak
2. tarja
3. hátszín
4. rostélyos
5. hátsó comb
6. stefánia
7. szegy
8. vastag lapocka
9. lábszár

pork/disznó

1. comb
2. karaj
3. tarja
4. dagadó + oldalas
5. lapocka
6. csülök

mutton/bárány or birka

1. comb
2. hátszín
3. nyak
4. szegy
5. lapocka

Meat

ESSENTIAL INFORMATION

- Key words to look for:
  HENTES (butcher or butcher's)
- Weight guide: 4-6 oz/125-200 g (15-20 dekagram) of meat per person for one meal.
- The diagrams opposite are to help you make sense of labels on counters and supermarket displays, and decide which cut or joint to have. Translations do not help, and you don't need to say the Hungarian word involved.
- You will find that lamb and especially mutton are less popular in Hungary. The butcher's display will tell you what's available.

WHAT TO SAY

For a joint, choose the type of meat and then say how many people it is for:

Some beef, please	**Marhahúst kérek** mor-ho-hoosht kairek
Some lamb	**Bárányt kérek** baa-raanjt kairek
Some pork	**Disznóhúst kérek** disnow-hoosht kairek
Some veal	**Borjúhúst kérek** bowr-yoo-hoosht kairek
A joint ...	**Egy darab húst kérek** edj dorob hoosht kairek
for two people	**két személy számára** kait seh-may saw-maw-roh
for four people	**négy személy számára** naidj seh-may saw-maw-roh

For steak, liver or kidney, do as above:

Some steak, please	**Egy szelet marhát kérek** edj selet mor-haat kairek
Some liver	**Májat kérek** maa-yot kairek
Some kidney	**Vesét kérek** ve-shayt kairek
Some sausages	**Kolbászt kérek** kowl-baast kairek
Some minced meat	**Darált húst kérek** doraalt hoosht kairek
for three people	**három személy számára** haa-rom seh-may saah-maah-roh
for five people	**öt személy számára** öt seh-may saah-maah-roh

For chops, do it this way:

Two veal escalopes, please	**Két borjúszeletet kérek** kait bowr-yoo-seletet kairek
Three pork chops	**Három szelet disznóhúst kérek** haa-rom selet deesnow-hoosht kairek
Five lamb chops	**Öt szelet bárányt kérek** öt selet baah-raanjt kairek

You may also want:

A chicken	**Egy csirkét kérek** edj cheer-kayt kairek
A tongue	**Kérek egy marhanyelvet** kairek edj morho-njelvet

[Other essential expressions see also p. 56.*]*

Please can you ...	**Megkérem, hogy ...** meg-kairem, hodj ...
mince it?	**darálja meg** doh-raal-yoh meg
dice it?	**vágja apróra** vaag-yah oprow-roh
trim the fat?	**tisztítsa meg a zsírtól** tisteet-shoh meg aw zheer-towl

Fish

ESSENTIAL INFORMATION

- The place to ask for: **HALAS**
  (Note: there are practically no "fish shops" in Hungary — fish is sold at the butcher's. Supermarkets usually have frozen fish.)
- The choice is usually limited to local fresh water fish. Shellfish, shrimp and other sea food is not part of the Hungarian cuisine.
- Large markets usually have fresh fish stalls.
- Weight guide: 8 oz/250 g (25 deka) minimum per person, for one meal of fish bought on the bone.

i.e.	1/2 kilo	for two people
	1 kilo	for four people
	1.5 kilo	for six people

Fish in Hungary is usually purchased in slices:

One slice of ...	**Kérek egy szelet ...**
	kairek edj selet ...
Two slices of ...	**Kérek két szelet ...**
	kairek kait selet ...
Six slices of ...	**Kérek hat szelet ...**
	kairek hot selet ...
carp	**ponty(ot)**
	powntj(owt)
wels	**harcsá(t)**
	horchaa(t)
cod	**tonhal(at)**
	ton-hol(ot)
(a carp-like, lean fresh-water fish)	**busá(t)**
	boo-shaa(t)

For some smaller fish specify the number you want:

A trout, please	**Egy pisztrángot kérek**
	edj pees-traangot kairek
A pikeperch, please	**Egy fogast kérek**
	edj fow-gosht kairek
A pike, please	**Egy csukát kérek**
	edj choo-kaat kairek
A bream, please	**Egy keszeget kérek**
	edj keseh-ghet kairek
A walleye, please	**Egy süllőt kérek**
	edj shool-löt kairek

[Other essential expressions see also p. 56.]

Please, can you ...	**Megkérem, hogy ...**
	meg-kairem, hodj ...
take the heads off?	**vágja le a fejét és a farkát**
	vaagh-yoh le aw feyait aish
	aw for-kaat
clean them?	**tisztítsa meg**
	tisteet-shoh megh
fillet them?	**filézze ki**
	filaiz-zeh kee

Eating and drinking out

Ordering a drink

ESSENTIAL INFORMATION

- The place to ask for:
  ESZPRESSZÓ (a kind of café)
  BOROZÓ (a wine bar)
  SÖRÖZŐ (a beer hall)
  VENDÉGLŐ (a restaurant)
  BÜFÉ (a simple bar)
- There is always waiter service in cafés, restaurants and beer halls.
- A service charge is almost always included on the bill even if not marked separately but it is customary to leave a tip of 10%.
- Restaurants and beer halls usually display their price list by the entrance or in the window.
- All these places usually serve nonalcoholic and alcoholic drinks as well. Cafés and simple bars are normally open all day.
- Coffee in Hungary is usually the thick and strong Italian-type "espresso" and it comes in small cups. Most places have milk or cream to dilute it.

WHAT TO SAY

I'll have ... please	**Kérek ...**
	kairek ...
a black coffee	**egy kávét**
	edj kaah-vayt
with cream	**tejszínnel**
	tey-seen-nel
a tea	egy **teát**
	edj tey-aat
with milk	**tejjel**
	teh-yel
with lemon	**citrommal**
	tsit-rom-mol

a glass of milk	**egy pohár tejet**
	edj poh-haar teh-yeht
two glasses of milk	**két pohár tejet**
	kait poh-haar teh-yet
a hot chocolate	**egy forró csokoládét**
	edj fowr-row chokoh-laah-dayt
a glass of mineral water	**egy ásványvizet**
	edj aash-vaanj-vee-zet
a lemonade	**egy limonádét**
	edj leemow-naa-dayt
a Coca Cola	**egy Coca Colát**
	edj Kow-koh Kow-laat
an orangeade	**egy narancs szörpöt**
	edj noronch sör-pöt
a fresh orange juice	**egy narancslevet**
	edj no-ronch-leh-veht
a grape juice	**egy szőlőlevet**
	edj söh-löh-levet
an apple juice	**egy almalevet**
	edj ol-mah-levet
a beer	**egy sört**
	edj shört
a draught beer	**egy csapolt sört**
	edj chop-owlt shört
a large beer	**egy korsó sört**
	edj kowr-show shört
a half	**egy pohár sört**
	edj pow-haar shört
A glass of ...	**Egy pohár ...**
	edj pow-haar ...
Two glasses of ...	**Két pohár ...**
	kait pow-haar ...
red wine	**vörösbort**
	vöh-rösh-bowrt
white wine	**fehérbort**
	fahair-bowrt
rosé wine	**rozét**
	row-zayt
dry	**száraz**
	saa-roz
sweet	**édes**
	aid-esh

A bottle of ...
Egy üveg ...
edj oovegh ...

    sparkling wine
pezsgő
pezh-göh

    champagne (French)
francia pezsgő
fron-tsee-ah pezh-göh

    champagne (Hungarian)
magyar pezsgő
modjor pezh-göh

A whisky
egy whisky
edj wisky

    with ice
jéggel
yaig-ghel

    with water
vízzel
veez-zel

    with soda
szódával
sow-daah-vol

A gin
egy gin
edj dzhin

    with tonic
tonikkal
tonik-kol

    with bitter lemon
(keserű) citrommal
(keshe-roo) tsit-rom-mol

A brandy/cognac
konyak
kow-njok

A Martini
egy martini/vermut
edj mortee-ny/ver-moot

A sherry
egy sherry
edj sherry

These are local drinks you may like to try:

pálinka
paah-lin-koh
a strong spirit distilled from
    various fruits

unikum
oony-koom
a bitter

tokaji
tow-kaw-yee
the classic Hungarian wine;
    sweet and dry variety

likőr
lee-kör
a sweet spirit

Other essential expressions:

Miss! *[This does not sound abrupt in Hungarian]*	**Kisasszony!** Keesh-os-sonj!
Waiter!	**Főúr!** Föh-oor!
The bill, please	**Fizetek** Fee-zetek
How much does that come to?	**Mennyi lesz?** Menj-njee less?
Is service included?	**A kiszolgálás benne van?** Aw kee-sol-gaah-laash ben-neh von?
Where is the toilet, please?	**Hol van a mosdó?** Howl von aw mosh-dow?

Ordering a snack

ESSENTIAL INFORMATION

- Look for any of these places:
  BÜFÉ (snack bar)
  FALATOZÓ (snack bar)
  PECSENYESÜTŐ (sausage and grill stall)
  LÁNGOS (a pancake fried in oil)
  SÖRÖZŐ (a beer hall or pub)
- Apart from snacks, most of these places serve soft drinks and beer.
- Look for the names of snacks (listed below) on signs in the stall or window.
- For cakes, *see p. 61.*
- For ice-cream, *see p. 62.*
- For picnic-type snacks, *see p. 66.*

WHAT TO SAY

I'll have ... please	Kérek egy ...
	kairek edj ...
a cheese sandwich/roll	**sajtos szendvicset/zsömlét**
	shoy-tosh send-vee-chet /zhöm-lait
a ham sandwich/roll	**sonkás szendvicset/zsömlét**
	shon-kaash send-vee-chet /zhöm-lait
an omelet	**omlettet**
	owm-let-tet
with diced ham	**sonkával**
	shon-kaah-vol

There are some other snacks you may like to try:

egy pár virsli	two Frankfurters
edj paar virsh-ly	
debreceni	a fried, spicy pork sausage
debreh-tseny	
sült kolbász	grilled sausage
shoolt-kowl-baas	
tükörtojás	fried eggs
tookör-tow-yaash	
bableves	spicy bean soup with pork knuckles
bob-levesh	
gulyás	spicy beef soup
ghoo-yaash	
lángos	pancake fried in oil
laan-gosh	

You may want to add to your order:

with bread, please	**kenyérrel**
	kenj-air-rel
with chips	**sült krumplival**
	shoolt-kroomply-vol
with potato salad	**burgonyasalátával**
	boor-gownjoh-shaw-laah-taah-vol
with mustard	**mustárral**
	moosh-taar-rol
with ketchup	**kecsappal**
	kechop-pol
with mayonnaise	**majonézzel**
	moyono-aiz-zel

[For other essential expressions, see "Ordering a drink", p. 76.]

In a restaurant

ESSENTIAL INFORMATION

- The place to ask for:
  VENDÉGLŐ
  ÉTTEREM
  SÖRÖZŐ (beer hall with limited choice)
  ÖNKISZOLGÁLÓ (ÉTTEREM/VENDÉGLŐ) (self service
  restaurant)
- The menu is usually displayed outside or in the window so that
  you can judge if the place is right for you.
- Most places have waiter service.
- It is usual to leave/give a tip (add it to the bill) of 10-15%.
- Most restaurants offer small portions for children. Look for:
  GYERMEK MENÜ (children's)
  KISADAG (small portion)
  ZÓNAÉTELEK (small portions not served during lunch or
  dinner time)
- Hot meals are served usually from 12.00 to 2.00 at lunchtime
  and from 6.00 to 9.00-10.00 at night. After that many restaurants
  offer snacks for latecomers (soups, sausages, salads, "zóna"
  dishes, etc.)

WHAT TO SAY

May I book a table?	**Szeretnék asztalt foglalni**
	seret-naik ostolt fowg-lol-ny
I've booked a table	**Van asztalfoglalásom**
	von ostol-fowg-low-laah-shom
A table ...	**Egy asztal ...**
	edj ostol ...
for one	**egy személyre**
	edj se-may-reh
for three	**három személyre**
	haarom se-may-reh
The menu, please	**Kérem az étlapot**
	kairem os ait-lopot
What's this, please?	**Ez micsoda, kérem?**
[point to menu]	es mee-chow-doh, kairem?

The wine list	**Az itallap**
	Oz ee-tol-lop
(200cc) of wine	**Két deci (200 cc) bor**
	Kait dey-tsy (200 cc) bowr
A half (500cc) liter wine	**Fél liter bor**
	Fail lee-ter bowr
A bottle	**Egy üveg**
	Edj oovegh
A glass	**Egy pohár** (100 or 200 cc)
	Edj pow-haar
A liter	**Egy liter**
	Egy lee-ter
red	**vörös**
	vöh-rösh
white	**fehér**
	feh-air
rosé	**rozé**
	row-zay
house wine	**folyó bor**
	fow-yow bowr
Some more bread, please	**Még egy kis kenyeret kérek**
	Maig edj kish kenj-eret kairek
Some more wine	**Még kérek bort**
	Maig kairek bowrt
Some oil	**Olajat kérek**
	Ow-low-yot kairek
Some vinegar	**Ecetet kérek**
	Et-setet kairek
Some salt	**Sót kérek**
	Showt kairek
Some pepper	**Borsot kérek**
	Bowr-shot kairek
Some water	**Vizet kérek**
	Vee-zet kairek
How much does that come to?	**Mennyi lesz ez összesen?**
	Menj-njee less ez ös-seshen?
Where is the toilet, please?	**Hol van a mosdó?**
	Howl von aw mowsh-dow?
Miss! [This does not sound abrupt in Hungarian]	**Kisasszony!**
	Keesh-os-sonj!
Waiter!	**Főúr!**
	Föh-oor!
The bill, please!	**Fizetek!**
	Fee-zetek!

Key words for courses, as seen on some menus:
[Only ask this question if you want the waiter to remind you of the choice.]

What have you got in the way of ...?	**Milyen ... van?**
	mee-yen ... von?
starters?	**előétel**
	eh-löh-aitel
soup?	**leves**
	levesh
fish?	**hal**
	hol
meat?	**hús**
	hoosh
game?	**vad**
	vod
fowl?	**szárnyas**
	saar-njosh
vegetables?	**zöldség**
	zöld-shaig
cheese?	**sajt**
	shoyt
fruit?	**gyümölcs**
	djoo-mölch
ice-cream?	**fagylalt**
	fodj-lolt
dessert?	**édesség**
	aidesh-shaig

UNDERSTANDING THE MENU

You will find the names of the principal ingredients of most dishes on these pages:

Starters, *see p. 76.*   Ice-cream, *see p. 62.*
Meat, *see p. 72.*   Fruit, *see p. 68.*
Fish, *see p. 74.*   Dessert, *see p. 61.*
Vegetables, *see p. 68.*   Cheese, *see p. 67.*

Used together with the following lists of cooking and menu terms, they should help you to decode the menu.
(These cooking and menu terms are for understanding only — not for speaking aloud.)

Cooking and menu terms

erőleves	broth, clear soup
sült	fried, roast — also joint
vajas	with butter
párolt	steamed
roston	grilled
főtt	boiled
vegyes	mixed
pácolt	pickled
füstölt	smoked
reszelt	grated
pirított	braised
pörkölt	stewed
rántott	in breadcrumbs
házi	homemade
hidegtál	cold cuts
jóasszony módra	with vegetables, sour cream and onions
vadász módra	in red wine sauce with mushrooms
befőtt	stewed fruit
püré	mashed
tejfeles	with sour cream
tejszín	cream
szelet	escalope
mustár	mustard
mártás	sauce

Further words to help you understand the menu

sült burgonya	fried potatoes
csülök	pig's knuckle
kacsa	duck
fácán	pheasant
pisztráng	trout
fogas	(a fish fried in whole)
fejes saláta	lettuce
tavaszi leves	fresh vegetable soup
parfé	ice-cream speciality
galuska	dumplings
burgonyafánk	small potato pancakes, fried
töltött káposzta	cabbage stuffed with minced meat

káposzta	cabbage
májgaluska	liver dumplings (in clear soup)
bableves	rich bean soup with smoked pork
zöldpaprika	green/white peppers
palacsinta	pancake
kolbász	spicy, smoked pork sausage
kelbimbó	Brussels sprouts
főtt burgonya	boiled potatoes
cékla	beetroot
csemege uborka	gherkins (pickled)
spárga	asparagus
tészta	pasta (also: cakes)
édesség	sweets
pulyka	turkey
bécsi szelet	veal escalope in breadcrumbs
zöldség	vegetables
erős paprika	red hot peppers
csípős	hot

Health

ESSENTIAL INFORMATION

- For details of reciprocal health agreements between your country and the country you are visiting, visit your local Department of Health office at least one month before leaving, or ask your travel agent.
- In addition, it is preferable to purchase a medical insurance policy through the travel agent, a broker or a motoring organization.
- Take your own "first-line" first aid kit with you.
- For minor disorders, and treatment at a drugstore, see p. 42.
- For finding your own way to a doctor, dentist, drugstore, see p. 20.
- Decide on a definite plan of action in case of serious illness: communicate your problem to a near neighbor, the receptionist or someone you see regularly. You are then dependent on that person helping you obtain treatment.
- For an ambulance (in Budapest only) call: 04
- If you need a doctor look for:
  KÓRHÁZ (hospital)
  ORVOSI RENDELŐ (dispensary)
  ORVOS (doctor)
  ELSŐSEGÉLY (first aid)
  BALESETI OSZTÁLY or **SEBÉSZET** (emergency department or surgery in a hospital)

What's the matter?

I have a pain in my ...	**Fáj a ...** faay aw ...
abdomen	**hasam** hoshom
ankle	**bokám** bow-kaam
arm	**karom** ko-rowm
back	**hátam** haah-tom

bladder	**hólyagom**
	how-yogom
bowels	**belem**
	belem
breast	**mellem**
	mel-lem
chest	**mellkasom**
	mell-koshom
ear	**fülem**
	foo-lem
eye	**szemem**
	semem
foot	**lábfejem**
	laab-feyem
head	**fejem**
	fe-yem
heel	**sarkam**
	shor-kom
jaw	**állam**
	aal-lom
kidneys	**vesém**
	ve-shaim
leg	**lábam**
	laa-bom
lung	**tüdőm**
	too-döm
neck	**nyakam**
	njok-om
penis	**péniszem**
	painis-em
shoulder	**vállam**
	vaal-om
stomach	**gyomrom**
	djom-rowm
testicles	**herém**
	heh-raim
throat	**torkom**
	towr-kowm
vagina	**vaginám**
	vo-ghee-naam
wrist	**csuklóm**
	chook-lowm
I have a pain here *[point]*	**Itt fáj**
	ett faay

I have a toothache	**Fáj a fogam**
	faay aw fow-gom
I have broken my denture	**Eltörött a fogsorom**
	el-töh-röt aw fowg-shorom
I have broken my glasses	**Eltörött a szemüvegem**
	el-töh-röt aw sem-oovegem
I have lost my contact lenses	**Elvesztettem a kontaktlencsémet**
	el-vestet-tem aw kown-tokt-lenchaimet
I have lost a filling	**Kiesett egy tömésem**
	kee-eshett edj töh-maishem
My child is ill	**Beteg a gyerekem**
	be-tegh aw djereh-kem
He/she has a pain **in his/her...**	**Fáj a ...**
	faay aw ...
ankle [see list above]	**bokája**
	bow-kaah-yoh

How bad is it?

I'm ill	**Beteg vagyok**
	be-tegh vo-djok
It's urgent	**Sürgős**
	shoor-gösh
It's serious	**Nagyon komoly**
	no-djon ko-mowy
It's not serious	**Nem komoly**
	nem ko-mowy
It hurts	**Fáj**
	faay
It hurts a lot	**Nagyon fáj**
	no-djon faay
It doesn't hurt much	**Nem nagyon fáj**
	nem no-djon faay
The pain occurs ...	**A fájdalom visszatér ...**
	aw faay-dolom vees-saw-tair...
every quarter of an hour	**minden negyedórában**
	men-den nedj-edow-raabon
every half hour	**minden félórában**
	men-den fail-owr-aabon
every hour	**minden órában**
	men-den owr-aabon
every day	**mindennap**
	meen-den-nop

most of the time	**folyton** fowy-ton
I've had it for...	**Már ...** maar ...
one hour/one day	**egy órája/egy napja** edj owr-aayoh/edj nop-yoh
two hours/two days	**két órája/két napja** kait owr-aayoh/kait nop-yoh
It's a ...	**Ez egy ...** es edj ...
sharp pain	**szúró fájdalom** soo-row faay-dolom
dull ache	**tompa fájdalom** towm-poh faay-dolom
nagging pain	**görcsös fájdalom** gör-chösh faay-dolom
I feel dizzy	**Szédülök** say-doolök
I feel sick	**Émelygést érzek** aim-ey-gaisht air-zek
I feel weak	**Gyenge vagyok** djen-ghe vodj-ok
I feel feverish	**Azt hiszem, lázam van** ost heesem, laaz-om von

Already under treatment for something else?

I take ... regularly [show]	**Rendszeresen szedem ...** rend-sereh-shen sedem ...
this medicine	**ezt az orvosságot** est oz owr-vosh-shaagot
these tablets	**ezt a tablettát** est ow tob-let-taat
I have ... a heart condition	**szívbeteg vagyok** seev-betegh vodj-ok
hemorrhoids	**aranyerem van** oronj-erem von
rheumatism	**reumás vagyok** reh-oomaash vodj-ok
I'm ...	**... vagyok** ... vodj-ok
diabetic	**cukorbeteg** tsoo-kowr-betegh

asthmatic	**asztmás**
	ost-maash
pregnant	**terhes**
	ter-hesh
allergic to (penicillin)	**allergiás (penicilinre)**
	ol-ler-ghee-aash (peny-tsy-lyn-reh)

Other essential expressions

Please, can you help?	**Kérem, segítsen**
	kairem, sheh-gheet-shen
A doctor, please	**Orvost keresek**
	owr-vosht kereh-shek
A dentist	**Fogorvost keresek**
	fowg-owr-vosht kereh-shek
I don't speak Hungarian	**Nem értek magyarul**
	nem air-tek modj-oh-rool
What time does ... arrive?	**Mikor jön meg ...?**
	meekor yön megh ...?
the doctor	**az orvos**
	oz owr-vosh
the dentist	**a fogorvos**
	aw fowg-owr-vosh

From the doctor: key sentences to understand

Take this ...	**Ezt szedje ...**
	est sed-yeh ...
every day/hour	**mindennap/órában**
	meen-den-nop/owr-aabon
twice/three times a day	**naponta kétszer/háromszor**
	nopon-toh kait-ser/haarom-sor
Stay in bed	**Maradjon ágyban**
	morod-yon aadj-bon
Don't travel . .	**Ne utazzon el ...**
	neh ootoz-zown el
for ... days/week	**még ... napig/hétig**
	maig ... nop-egh/hait-egh
You must go to hospital	**Be kell feküdnie a kórházba**
	beh kell fe-kood-ny-eh aw kowr-haaz-boh

Problems: complaints, loss, theft

ESSENTIAL INFORMATION

- Problems with:
  camping facilities, *see p. 36.*
  health, *p. 87.*
  household appliances, *see p. 39.*
  the car, *see p. 103.*
- If the worst comes to the worst, find the police station.
  To ask the way, *see p. 20.*
- Look for:
  RENDŐRSÉG (police)
- Ask for:
  TALÁLT TÁRGYAK (lost property — public transport only)
- If you lose your passport, go to your nearest consulate.
- In an emergency dial 07 (for police) or 04 (ambulance) or 05 (if
  there is a fire). These phone numbers for Budapest only: outside
  the capital check individually for each city.

COMPLAINTS

I bought this ...	**... vásároltam ezt**
	... vaash-aah-rol-tom est
today	**ma**
	moh
yesterday	**tegnap**
	tegh-nop
on Monday *[see p. 125.]*	**hétfőn**
	hait-fön
It's no good	**Nem jó**
	nem yow
Look	**Nézze**
	naiz-zeh
Here *[point]*	**Itt**
	eet
Can you ...	**Nem lehetne ...**
	nem lehetne ...
change it?	**kicserélni?**
	kee-cherail-ny?
mend it?	**megjavítani?**
	megh-yaw-veetoh-ny?

Here's the receipt	**Itt van a blokk**
	eet von aw blowk
Can I have a refund?	**Kérem vissza a pénzt**
	kairem vees-soh aw painzt
Can I see the manager?	**A vezetővel akarok beszélni**
	aw vez-etöh-vel okoh-rowk beh-sail-ny

LOSS
[See also "Theft" below: the lists are interchangeable]

I've lost ...	**Elvesztettem ...**
	elves-tet-tem ...
my bag	**a táskámat**
	aw taash-kaam-ot
my bracelet	**a karkötőmet**
	aw kor-köh-töh-met
my camera	**a fényképezőgépemet**
	aw fainj-kaip-ezöh-gaip-eh-met
my car keys	**az autókulcsomat**
	oz oh-ootow-kool-chom-ot
my car logbook	**a forgalmi engedélyt**
	aw fowr-golmy engeh-dayt
my driving license	**a jogosítványomat**
	aw yowg-owsh-eet-vaanj-owmot
my insurance certificate	**a biztosítási papírjaimat**
	aw beez-tosh-eet-aashy poh-peer-yo-eemot
my jewellery	**az ékszeremet**
	oz aik-seremet
my keys	**a kulcsomat**
	aw kool-chomot
everything!	**mindent!**
	meen-dent!

THEFT
[See also "Loss" above: the lists are interchangeable]

Someone has stolen ...	**Ellopták ...**
	el-lowp-taak ...
my car	**az autómat**
	oz oh-ootow-mot
my car radio	**az autórádiómat**
	oz ah-ootow-raah-dee-owm-ot

my money	**a pénzemet**
	aw pain-zemet
my necklace	**a nyakláncomat**
	aw njok-laan-tsomot
my passport	**az útlevelemet**
	oz oot-leveh-lemet
my radio	**a rádiómat**
	aw raah-dee-owm-ot
my tickets	**a jegyemet**
	aw yedj-emet
my traveler's checks	**az úticsekkemet**
	oz ooty-chek-kemet
my wallet	**a tárcámat**
	aw taar-tsaam-ot
my watch	**az órámat**
	oz owr-aam-ot
my luggage	**a poggyászomat**
	aw powdj-djaas-owm-ot

LIKELY REACTIONS: key words to understand

Wait	**Várjon**
	vaar-yon
When?	**Mikor?**
	mee-kowr?
Where?	**Hol?**
	hol?
Your name?	**Neve?**
	neh-veh?
Address?	**Lakcím?**
	lok-tseem?
I can't help you	**Nem tudok segíteni**
	nem tood-ok shegeet-eh-ny
Nothing to do with me	**Nem rám tartozik**
	nem raam tor-towz-eek

The post office

ESSENTIAL INFORMATION

- To find a post office, *see p. 20.*
- Key words to look for:
  POSTA
  POSTAHIVATAL
- For stamps, look for the word **BÉLYEG**
- Some stationeries and kiosks (also tobacconists) which sell postcards also sell stamps.
- Mailboxes in Hungary are red. An inserted label on some mailboxes indicates when they are emptied.
- Plain stamped postcards and stamps can also be obtained from vending machines at some post offices.
- For *poste restante* you should show your passport at the counter marked **POSTE RESTANTE** or **POSTÁN MARADÓ KÜLDEMÉNYEK.** A small fee may be payable.

WHAT TO SAY

To England, please	**Angliába, kérem** ong-lee-aah-boh, kairem

[Hand letters, cards or parcels over the counter]

To Australia	**Ausztráliába** aw-oost-raaly-aah-boh
To the United States	**Az Egyesült Államokba** oz eh-djeh-shoolt aal-lom-owk-boh

[For other countries, see p. 129.]

How much is ...?	**Mennyibe kerül...?** menj-njee-beh ker-ool ...?
this parcel (to Canada)	**ez a csomag (Kanadába)** ez aw chow-mog (ko-naw-daah-bah)
a letter (to Australia)	**egy levél (Ausztráliába)** edj le-vail (Aw-oost-raaly-aah-boh)

a postcard (to England)	**egy levelezőlap (Angliába)** edj leveleh-zöh-lop (Ong-lee-aah-boh)
Airmail	**Légiposta** lay-ghee-powsh-toh
Surface mail	**Normál tarifa** nowr-maal toree-foh
One stamp, please	**Egy bélyeget kérek** edj bay-eghet kairek
Two stamps, please	**Két bélyeget kérek** kait bay-eghet kairek
One (6) forint stamp	**Egy (6) forintos bélyeg** edj (hot) fowr-intosh bay-eg
I'd like to send a telegram	**Táviratot szeretnék küldeni** taah-vee-rotot seret-naik kool-deh-nee

Telephoning

ESSENTIAL INFORMATION

- Public phone boxes (**NYILVÁNOS TÁVBESZÉLŐ ÁL-LOMÁS** or **TELEFONFÜLKE**) are usually painted yellow and take coins. Foreign calls can only be made from boxes that display the words **NEMZETKÖZI HÍVÁSOK** and/or instructions in foreign languages.
  This is how to use a public telephone:
  — take off the receiver
  — wait for the dial tone
  — insert the coins
  — dial the number
- For international calls dial first 00 and wait for a second dial tone before dialing through the country and area code plus the local number you want to reach.
  For long distance calls within Hungary dial first 06 and wait for a second dial tone before dialing through the area code and the local number. The area code for Budapest is (1).
- If you need a number abroad ring inquiries (**NEMZETKÖZI TUDAKOZÓ**) Budapest 1186-977 from 7-20 hours on workdays. They normally speak English.
- There is also a foreign language inquiry service: Budapest 1172-200
- For calls to countries which cannot be dialed direct go to a post office and write the country, town and number you want on a piece of paper. Add **MEGHÍVÁSSAL** if you want a person-to-person call or **R-BESZÉLGETÉS** if you want to reverse the charges.
- If you have difficulty in making a phone call, go to the post office and get them to put the call through (see above).

WHAT TO SAY

Where can I make a telephone call?	**Hol lehet telefonálni?** hol leh-het teleh-fown-aal-ny?
Local	**Helyi beszélgetés** hey-ee beh-sail-getaish
Abroad	**Nemzetközi hívás** nemzet-köh-zee hee-vaash

I'd like this number ...   **Ezt a számot kérem ...**
[show number]   est aw saam-ot kairem ...
   in England   **Angliában**
       ong-lee-aah-bon

   in Canada   **Kanadában**
       konoh-daah-bon

   in the USA   **az USA-ban**
       az ooshaah-bon

[For other countries, see p. 129.]

Can you dial it for me, please?   **Hívja fel nekem, kérem ...**
       heev-yoh fel nekem, kairem ...

How much is it?   **Mennyibe kerül?**
       menj-njee-beh kerool?

Hello!   **Halló!**
       hol-low!

May I speak to ...?   **... kérem**
       ... kairem

Extension   **... mellék**
       ... mel-laik

I'm sorry, I don't speak   **Sajnos, nem tudok magyarul**
   Hungarian   shoy-nosh. nem toodok
       modjor-ool

Do you speak English?   **Tud ön angolul?**
       tood ön ong-owl-ool?

Thank you, I'll phone back   **Köszönöm, újra fogom hívni**
       köh-söh-nöm, ooy-roh fow-gowm
       heev-ny

Good-bye   **Viszontlátásra**
       vee-sont-laat-aash-roh

LIKELY REACTIONS

That's (10) forints (50)   **(10) forint (50) lesz**
       (teez) fowr-int (öt-ven) less

Cabin number (3)   **(3) fülke**
       (haar-mosh) fool-keh

[For numbers, see p. 121.]

Don't hang up   **Ne tegye le**
       neh tedj-eh leh

I'm trying to connect you   **Kapcsolom**
       kop-chowl-om

You are through	**Tessék beszélni**
	tesh-shaik beh-sail-ny
There's a delay	**Várni kell**
	vor-nee kell
I'll try again	**Később újra megpróbálom**
	kaish-öbb ooy-roh meg-prowb-aal-om

Changing checks and money

ESSENTIAL INFORMATION

- Finding your way to a bank or change bureau, *see p. 20.*
- Look for these words:
  BANK
  TAKARÉKPÉNZTÁR (savings bank)
  PÉNZVÁLTÁS (change bureau)
- Banks are normally open from 8/9.00 a.m. to 3/4.00 p.m. on weekdays.
- Change bureaux at frontier posts, airports and larger railway stations, also some hotels and tourist offices are usually open outside regular banking hours.
- Changing money or traveler's checks (in banks) is usually a two-stage process. The formalities are completed at a desk called **PÉNZVÁLTÁS** or **DEVIZÁK** and then you will be sent to the cashier (**PÉNZTÁR**) to get your money.
- Credit cards are accepted at all better shops and restaurants; they usually display the signs in the window. Write in English.
- Have your passport handy.

WHAT TO SAY

I'd like to cash ...	**Szeretném beváltani...**
	seret-naim beh-vaal-tony ...
this traveler's check	**ezt az úticsekket**
	est oz ooty-chek-ket
these traveler's checks	**ezeket az úticsekkeket**
	ezeh-ket oz ooty-chek-keket
this check	**ezt a csekket**
	est aw chek-ket
I'd like to change this into Forint	**Szeretném ezt a pénzt forintra váltani**
	seret-naim est aw painzt fow-rint-roh vaal-tony
Here's ...	**Tessék ...**
	tesh-shaik ...
my credit card	**a hitelkártyám**
	aw heetel-kaart-yaam

my passport   **az útlevelem**
oz oot-leveh-lem

What is the rate of exchange?   **Mi az átváltási árfolyam?**
mee oz aat-vaal-taashy aar-
foh-yom?

LIKELY REACTIONS

Your passport, please   **Az útlevelét kérem**
oz oot-leveh-lait kairem

Sign here   **Itt tessék aláírni**
eet tesh-shaik olaah-eerny

Your credit card, please   **Kérem a hitelkártyáját**
kairem aw heetel kaart-yaah-yaat

Go to the cash desk   **Fáradjon a pénztárhoz**
faar-odyon aw painz-taar-hoz

Car travel

ESSENTIAL INFORMATION

- Finding a filling station or garage, *see p. 20.*
- Is it a self-service station? Look out for:
  ÖNKISZOLGÁLÓ
  They are not very common.
- Grades of gasoline:
  NORMÁL (standard)
  SZUPER (premium)
  EXTRA (premium plus)
  DIESEL
  KEVERÉK (two-stroke)
- 1 gallon is about 4.5 liters (accurate enough up to 6 gallons).
- The minimum sale is often 5 liters.
- On familiar road signs and warnings, *see p. 117.*

WHAT TO SAY
[For numbers, see p. 121.]

(9) liters of ...	**(9) liter ...**
	(kee-lents) lee-ter ...
(500) forints of ...	**(500) forintért ...**
	(öt-saaz) fow-reen-tairt ...
standard	**normál**
	nowr-maal
premium	**szuper**
	soo-per
premium plus	**extra**
	eks-troh
diesel	**diesel**
	dee-zel
Fill it up, please	**Tele kérem**
	teh-leh kairem
Will you check ...	**Ellenőrizze, kérem ...**
	el-len-ör-eez-zeh, kairem ...
the oil	**az olajat**
	oz owl-oy-ot
the battery	**az akkumulátort**
	oz ok-koo-moo-laat-owrt

the radiator	**a hűtőt** aw hoot-öt
the tires	**a légnyomást** aw laig-njowm-aasht
I've run out of gas	**Kifogyott a benzinem** kee-fodj-owt aw ben-zee-nem
Can I borrow a can, please?	**Nem tudna kölcsön adni egy kannát?** nem tood-noh köl-chön odny edj kon-naat?
My car has broken down	**Lerobbant a kocsim** leh-rowb-bont aw kow-chim
My car won't start	**Nem akar elindulni a kocsim** nem okor el-een-doolny aw kow-chim
I've had an accident	**Balesetem volt** bol-eshet-tem vowlt
I've lost my car keys	**Elvesztettem a kocsi kulcsait** elves-tet-tem aw kow-chy kool- choh-eet
My car is ...	**A kocsim ...** aw kow-chim ...
one kilometer away	**egy kilométerre van innen** edj keelow-maiter-reh von een-nen
three kilometers away	**három kilométerre van innen** haa-rom keelow-maiter-reh von een-nen
Can you help me, please?	**Nem tudna segíteni, kérem?** nem tood-noh sheg-eeteny, kairem?
Do you do repairs?	**Vállalnak javítást?** vaal-lol-nok yaw-veetaasht?
I have a puncture	**Durrdefektem van** doorr-defek-tem von
I have a broken windscreen	**Betört a szélvédőm** beh-tört aw sail-vaid-öm
I don't know what's wrong	**Nem tudom, mi a baj** nem tood-owm, mee aw boy
I think the problem is here *[point]*	**Azt hiszem, itt van a baj** ost hee-sem, eet von aw boy

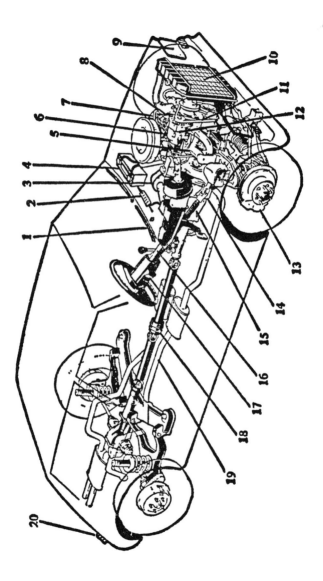

1 windscreen wipers	**ablaktörlő** oblok-tör-lő	
2 fuses	**biztosítékok** beez-toshy-taikok	
3 heater	**fűtés** foot-aish	
4 battery	**akkumulátor** ok-koomool-aator	
5 engine	**motor** mow-tor	
6 fuel pump	**benzinpumpa** benzeen-poom-poh	
7 starter	**motorindító** mow-tor-een-deetow	
8 carburetor	**porlasztó** powr-los-tow	
9 lights	**reflektor** ref-lektowr	
10 radiator	**hűtő** hoo-tőh	

11 fan belt	**ékszíj** aik-seey	
12 generator	**generátor** gheneh-raat-or	
13 brakes	**fék** faik	
14 clutch	**kuplung** koop-loong	
15 gear box	**sebességváltó** shebesh-shaig-vaal-tow	
16 steering	**volán** voh-laan	
17 ignition	**gyújtás** djooy-taash	
18 transmission	**kardántengely** kordaan-tenghey	
19 exhaust	**kipufogó** kee-poo-fogow	
20 indicators	**irányjelző** eeronj-yelzöh	

Can you ...
Nem tudná ...
nem tood-naw ...

repair the fault?
megjavítani a hibát?
megh-yoveet-ony aw hee-baat?

come and look?
megnézni?
megh-naizny?

estimate the cost?
megmondani, hogy mibe kerül?
megh-mown-dony, hodj mee-beh keh-rool?

write it down?
leírni?
leh-eerny?

How long will the repair take?
Meddig tart a javítás?
med-deegh tort aw yow-yeetosh?

When will the car be ready?
Mikor lesz készen a kocsi?
meekor less kaisen aw kow-chy?

Can I see the bill?
Megnézhetném a számlát?
megh-naiz-hetnaim aw saam-laat?

This is my insurance document
Ez a biztosítási kötvényem
es aw beez-toshy-taashy köt-vainj-em

HIRING A CAR

Can I hire a car?
Autót szeretnék bérelni
oh-ootowt seret-naik bair-elny

I need a car ...
... kell a kocsi
... kell aw kow-chy

for two people
két személyre
kait semay-reh

for five people
öt személyre
öt semay-reh

for one day
egy napra
edj nop-roh

for five days
öt napra
öt nop-roh

for a week
egy hétre
edj hait-reh

Can you write down ...
Nem tudná leírni, kérem ...
nem tood-noh leh-eerny, kairem

the deposit to pay?
mennyi letétet kell fizetni?
menj-njee leh-taitet kell feezet-ny

the charge per kilometer?
mennyi a díj kilométerenként?
menj-njee aw deey keelow-maiteren-kaint?

the daily charge?	**mennyi a díj naponként?** menj-njee aw deey nopon-kaint?
the cost of insurance?	**mibe kerül a biztosítás?** mee-beh keh-rool aw beez-toshy-taash?
Can I leave it in (Szeged)?	**Leadhatom (Szegeden)?** leh-od-howtom (seh-gheden)?
What documents do I need?	**Milyen iratokra van szükségem?** mee-yen eerotok-roh von sook-shaigem?

LIKELY REACTIONS

I don't do repairs	**Javítást nem vállalunk** yoveet-aasht nem vaal-loloonk
Where's your car?	**Hol van a kocsi?** hol von aw kow-chy?
What make is it?	**Milyen márka?** mee-yen maar-koh?
Come back tomorrow/ Monday	**Jöjjön vissza holnap/hétfőn** yöh-yön vees-soh hol-nop/hait-fön

[For days of the week, see p. 125.]

We don't hire cars	**Mi nem kölcsönzünk kocsit** me nem kö-chön-zoonk kow-chit
Your driving license, please	**A jogosítványát kérem** a yowgow-sheet-vaanj-aat kairem
The mileage is unlimited	**A kilométerszám nincs korlátozva** aw keelow-maiter-saam ninch kor-laat-oz-voh

Public transport

ESSENTIAL INFORMATION

- Finding the way to the bus station, a bus stop, a trolley stop, the railroad station and a taxi stand, *see p. 20*.
- Remember that lining up for buses is unheard of!
- There are several taxi companies and unions, each with a different phone center that are not linked; you can also hail cabs in the street.
- Types of trains:
  EXPRESSZ (long distance, often between countries, stopping only at principal stations)
  GYORSVONAT (fast train to and between regional centers, medium distance, stopping only at principal stations)
  SZEMÉLYVONAT (slow train, medium distance, stopping at all stations)
- Key words on signs:
  JEGY (ticket)
  PÉNZTÁR (ticket office)
  BEJÁRAT (entrance)
  KIJÁRAT (exit)
  TILOS (forbidden)
  VÁGÁNY (platform, literally: track)
  PERON (platform)
  ÁLLOMÁSFŐNÖK (head of station)
  TUDAKOZÓ (information)
  FELVILÁGOSÍTÁS (information)
  MÁV (initials of Hungarian railways)
  CSOMAGMEGŐRZŐ (checkroom)
  BUSZMEGÁLLÓ (bus stop)
  INDULÁS (timetable, departures)
  ÉRKEZÉS (timetable, arrivals)
  CSOMAGFELADÁS (luggage office/forwarding office)
  VONAT (train)
- Buying a ticket:
  Buy your train ticket and seat reservation at the ticket office inside the station or at certain travel agencies.
  When traveling by bus or streetcar or trolley or subway you have to use (punch with the machine inside the vehicle or, in case of the subway, at the entrance) tickets sold at end stations, main stations' ticket offices or some tobacconists. Bus tickets

and other tickets are different in color as bus rides are more expensive.

You have to use a new ticket for each ride!

In Budapest day-tickets — valid for all lines and types of transport — are available at end stations or main station ticket offices.

WHAT TO SAY

Where does the train for (Miskolc) leave?	**Melyik vágányról megy a vonat (Miskolcra)?**
	Meh-yeek vaah-gaanj-rowl medj aw vow-not (Mish-kowlts-row)?
At what time does the train leave for (Miskolc)?	**Mikor indul a vonat (Miskolcra)?**
	Mee-kowr indool aw vow-not (Mish-kowltc-row)?
At what time does the train arrive in (Miskolc)?	**Mikor érkezik a vonat (Miskolcra)?**
	Mee-kowr air-keh-zik aw vow-not (Mish-kowlts-row)?
Is this the train for (Miskolc)?	**Ez a vonat megy (Miskolcra)?**
	Ez aw vow-not medj (Mish-kowlts-row)?
Where does the bus leave for (Szeged)?	**Honnan indul a busz (Szegedre)?**
	Hon-non een-dool aw boos (Seghed-reh)?
At what time does the bus leave for (Szeged)?	**Mikor indul a busz (Szegedre)?**
	Mee-kor een-dool aw boos (Seghed-reh)?
At what time does the bus arrive at (Szeged)?	**Mikor érkezik a busz (Szegedre)?**
	Mee-kor air-keh-zik aw boos (Seghed-reh)?
Is this the bus for (Szeged)?	**Ez a busz megy (Szegedre)?**
	Ez aw boos medj (Seghed-reh)?
Do I have to change?	**Nem kell átszállnom?**
	Nem kell aat-saal-nowm?

Where does ... leave from?	**Honnan indul a ...?**
	hon-non een-dool aw ...?
the bus	**a busz**
	aw boos
the train	**a vonat**
	aw vow-not
the subway	**a metró**
	aw met-row
for the airport	**a repülőtérre**
	aw rep-poolöh-tair-reh
for the cathedral	**a templomhoz**
	aw tem-plowm-hoz
for the beach	**a strandra**
	aw shtrond-roh
for the marketplace	**a piacra**
	aw pee-ots-roh
for the railroad station	**a vasútállomásra**
	aw voshoot-aal-lowm-aash-roh
for the town center	**a városközpontba**
	aw vaah-rosh-köz-pont-boh
for the swimming pool	**az uszodába**
	oz oosow-daah-boh
Is this...	**Ez a ...**
	ez aw ...
the bus for the market-place?	**busz megy a piactérre?**
	boos medj aw pee-ots-tair-reh?
the streetcar for the railroad station?	**villamos megy a vasút-állomásra?**
	vil-lomosh medj aw voshoot-aal-lomaash-roh?
Where can I get a taxi?	**Hol kapok taxit?**
	hol kopok tok-seet?
Can you put me off at the right stop, please?	**Szóljon kérem, hol kell leszállnom**
	sowl-yon kairem, hol kell leh-saal-nom
Can I book a seat?	**Szeretnék helyjegyet váltani**
	seret-naik hey-yedj-et vaal-tony
A single	**Csak oda**
	chok owd-oh
A round-trip	**Retúrjegy**
	reh-toor-yedj
First class	**Első osztály**
	el-shöh ost-aay

Second class	**Másodosztály**
	Maashod-ost-aay
One adult	**Egy felnőtt**
	Edj fel-nöt
Two adults	**Két felnőtt**
	Kait fel-nöt
and one child	**És egy gyermek**
	Aish edj djer-mek
and two children	**És két gyermek**
	Ais kait djer-mek
How much is it?	**Mibe kerül?**
	Mee-beh keh-rool?

LIKELY REACTIONS

Over there	**Odaát**
	Ow-doh-aat
Here	**Itt**
	Eet
Platform (1)	**(Első) vágány**
	(El-shöh) vaah-gaanj
At (four) o'clock	**(Négy) órakor**
	(Naidj) ow-rokor
[For times, see p. 123.]	
Change at (Siófok)	**(Siófokon) szálljon át**
	(Shee-owf-okon) saal-yon aat
Change at (the main square)	**(A főtéren) szálljon át**
	(Aw föh-tairen) saal-yon aat
This is your stop	**Itt kell leszállni**
	Eet kel leh-saal-nee
There's only first class	**Csak első osztály van**
	Chok el-shöh ost-aay von
There's a supplement	**Pótdíjat kell fizetni**
	Powt-dee-yot kel fee-zet-nee

Leisure

ESSENTIAL INFORMATION

- Finding the way to the place of entertainment, *see p. 20.*
- For times of day, *see p. 123.*
- Important signs, *see p. 117.*
- In the more popular resorts, you pay to go on the beach and to rent a deck chair.
- Smoking is forbidden in theaters and movies.
- It is customary to leave one's coat at the cloakroom in theaters.

WHAT TO SAY

At what time does ... open?	**Mikor nyit ...?** mee-kor njeet ...?
the art gallery	**a képtár** aw kaip-taar
the botanical garden	**a botanikus kert** aw bowt-ony-koosh kert
the cinema	**a mozi** aw mow-zee
the concert hall	**a hangversenyterem** aw hong-vershenj-terem
the disco	**a diszkó** aw dis-kow
the museum	**a múzeum** aw moo-zeh-oom
the night club	**a bár** aw baar
the sports stadium	**a stadion** aw shto-dee-on
the swimming pool	**az uszoda** oz oosow-dah
the theater	**a színház** aw seen-haaz
the zoo	**az állatkert** oz all-lot-kert

At what time does ... close?	**Mikor zár ...?**
	mee-kor zaar ...?
the art gallery	**a képtár**
	aw kaip-taar
[See above list]	

At what time does ... start?	**Mikor kezdődik ...?**
	mee-kor kez-dö-dik ...?
the cabaret	**a kabaré**
	aw koh-boh-ray
the concert	**a hangverseny**
	aw hong-ver-shenj
the film	**a film**
	aw film
the match	**a meccs**
	aw mech
the play	**az előadás**
	oz eh-löh-odaash
the race	**a verseny**
	aw ver-shenj
How much is it ...?	**Mibe kerül ...?**
	mee-beh keh-rool?
for an adult	**egy felnőttjegy**
	edj fel-nöt-yedj
for a child	**egy gyerekjegy**
	edj djeh-rek-yedj
Two adults, please	**Két felnőttjegyet kérek**
	kait fel-nöt-yeh-djet kairek
Three children, please	**Három gyerekjegyet kérek**
	haa-rom djeh-rek-yeh-djet kairek
[State price, if there's a choice]	

Stalls/circle	**zsöllye/páholy**
	zhöh-yeh/paah-hoy
Do you have ... ?	**Nem tud adni...?**
	nem tood od-nee ...?
a program	**egy műsort**
	edj moo-short
a guidebook	**egy tájékoztatót**
	edj taah-yaik-oz-taw-towt
Where is the toilet, please?	**Hol van a mosdó?**
	hol von aw mosh-dow?
Where is the cloakroom?	**Hol van a ruhatár?**
	hol von aw roo-hoh-taar?

I would like lessons in ...	**Szeretnék ... leckét venni** seret-naik ... lets-kait ven-nee
skiing	**sí** shee
sailing	**vitorlázás** vee-tor-laaz-aash
water skiing	**vízisí** vee-zee-shee
wind-surfing	**szörf** sörf
Can I hire ...?	**Lehet itt ... kölcsönözni?** leh-het eet ... köl-chön-öz-nee
some skis	**sílécet** shee-laits-et
some ski boots	**sícipőt** shee-tsee-pöt
a boat	**csónakot** chow-nok-ot
a fishing rod	**horgászbotot** hor-gaas-botot
a deck chair	**nyugágyat** njoog-aadj-ot
the necessary equipment	**felszerelést** fel-ser-elaisht
How much is it ...?	**Mibe kerül ...?** mee-beh keh-rool ...?
per day/hour	**egy napra/órára** edj nop-roh/owr-aar-oh
Do I need a license?	**Nem kell hozzá igazolvány?** nem kell howz-zoh eegoz-owl-vonj?

Asking if things are allowed

ESSENTIAL INFORMATION

- May one smoke here?
  May I smoke here?
  Can one smoke here?   **Lehet itt dohányozni?**
  Can I smoke here?
  Is it possible to smoke here?
- All these English variations can be expressed in one way in Hungarian. To save space, only the first English version: "May one ...?" is shown below.

WHAT TO SAY

Excuse me, please	**Bocsánat**
	boh-chaa-not
May one ...?	**Lehet itt ...?**
	leh-het eet ...?
camp here	**sátorozni**
	shaa-towr-oznee
come in	**bejönni**
	beh-yöh-nee
dance here	**táncolni**
	taan-tsol-nee
fish here	**horgászni**
	hor-gaas-nee
get a drink here	**inni valamit**
	een-nee voloh-meet
get out this way	**kimenni**
	kee-men-nee
get something to eat here	**enni valamit**
	en-nee voloh-meet
leave one's thing here	**hagyni a holmit**
	hodj-nee aw hol-meet
look around	**körülnézni**
	körool-naiz-nee
park here	**parkolni**
	park-kowl-nee
picnic here	**piknikezni**
	peek-neek-ez-nee

sit here	**leülni**
	leh-ool-nee
smoke here	**dohányozni**
	dowh-haanj-oz-nee
swim here	**úszni**
	oos-nee
take photos here	**fényképezni**
	fainj-kaip-ez-nee
telephone here	**telefonálni**
	teleh-fown-aal-nee
wait here	**várakozni**
	vaar-okoz-nee

LIKELY REACTIONS

Yes, certainly	**Igen, természetesen**
	eeg-en, ter-maiset-eshen
Help yourself	**Tessék parancsolni**
	tesh-shaik poron-chowl-nee
I think so	**Azt hiszem**
	ozt hee-sem
Of course	**Persze**
	per-seh
Yes, but be careful	**Igen, de legyen óvatos**
	eeg-en, deh ledjen owv-otosh
No, certainly not	**Nem lehet**
	nem leh-het
I don't think so	**Nem hiszem**
	nem hee-sem
Not normally	**Általában nem**
	aal-tolaa-bon nem
Sorry	**Sajnálom, nem**
	shoy-naal-om. nem

Reference

PUBLIC NOTICES

Key words on signs for drivers, pedestrians, travelers, shoppers and overnight guests.

A KUTYA HARAP	Beware of the dog
ALAGSOR	Basement, lower ground floor
AUTOMATA CSOMAG-MEGŐRZŐ	Luggage lockers
AUTÓPÁLYA	Divided highway
ÁLLJ	Stop
ÁLLÓHELY	Standing room
ÁRLESZÁLLÍTÁS	Sale
ÁTMENŐ FORGALOM	Through traffic
BEHAJTANI TILOS	No through traffic
BEJÁRAT	Entrance
BELÉPŐJEGY	Admission (ticket)
CSOMAGMEGŐRZŐ	Checkroom
CSÚSZÁSVESZÉLY	Slippery surface (road)
DÍJ	Fees, charges
DOHÁNYZÓ	Smoking allowed
EGYIRÁNYÚ	One-way street
ELADÓ	For sale
ELFOGYOTT	Sold out
ELŐZNI TILOS	Passing forbidden
ELSŐSEGÉLY	First aid
EMELET (ELSŐ, MÁSO-DIK, HARMADIK)	Floor (first, second, third)
ÉPÍTÉSI TERÜLET	Building site
ÉRKEZÉS	Arrivals
ÉTKEZŐKOCSI	Dining car
FELJÁRAT	Entrance of divided highway
FELSZÁLLÁS	Enter (the bus)
FELTÉTELES MEGÁLLÓ	Bus stop on request
FELVILÁGOSÍTÁS	Information office
FÉRFIAK	Gentlemen
FOGLALT	Reserved
FÖLDSZINT	Ground floor
FÖLDÚT	Dirt road
FÜRDŐ	Bathroom

GARÁZS	Underground parking
GYORSSZOLGÁLAT	Fast service
HÁLÓKOCSI	Sleeper (railroad)
HEGYOMLÁS	Falling rocks
HÉTKÖZNAP	Working days
HIDEG	Cold (tap)
HIVATALOS IDŐ	Office hours
HORDÁR	Porter
HÚZNI	Pull
IDEGENVEZETŐ	Guide
INDULÁS	Departures
ISKOLA	School
IVÓVÍZ	Drinking water
JEGYPÉNZTÁR	Ticket office
JOBBRA TARTS	Keep right
KERÉKPÁRÚT	Bike path
KÉTIRÁNYÚ KÖZLE-KEDÉS	Two-way traffic
KIADÓ	For hire, for rent
KIÁRUSÍTÁS	Clearance sale
KIJÁRAT	Exit
KÓRHÁZ	Hospital
LASSAN HAJTS	Drive slowly, slow down
LIFT	Elevator
MAGÁN	Private
MAGÁNTERÜLET	Private grounds
MEGÉRINTENI TILOS	Do not touch
MELEG	Hot (tap)
METRO	Subway (train)
MOZGÓLÉPCSŐ	Escalator
NE ZAVARJ	Do not disturb
NEM BEJÁRAT	No entry
NEM DOHÁNYZÓ	Nonsmoker (compartment)
NŐK	Ladies
NYILVÁNOS	Public (phone, conveniences)
NYITVA	Open
NYITVATARTÁS	Opening hours
ÖNKISZOLGÁLÓ	Self service
ŐRZÖTT PARKOLÓ	Supervised car park
PARKOLÓ	Car park
PARKOLÓHÁZ	Multi-storey car park
PÉNZBEDOBÁS	Coin to put in
PÉNZTÁR	Cash desk
PERON	Platform

Notes

Notes

PRIVÁT	Access to residents only
PUHA ÚTPADKA	Soft shoulders
RECEPCIÓ	Reception
RENDKÍVÜLI AJÁNLAT	Special offer
RENDŐRSÉG	Police
SAJÁT FELELŐSSÉGÉRE	At one's own risk
SEBESSÉGKORLÁTOZÁS	Speed limit
SÉTÁLÓ UTCA	Pedestrian zone
SZABAD	Vacant (toilet)
SZOBA KIADÓ	Room to rent
SZÜNNAP	Closed all day
TALÁLT TÁRGYAK	Lost property
TÁVBESZÉLŐ ÁLLOMÁS	Public telephone
TERELŐÚT	Detour
TESSÉK CSÖNGETNI	Ring (bell)
TESSÉK KOPOGNI	Knock (door)
TILOS	Forbidden
TILOS A DOHÁNYZÁS	No smoking
TILOS A FÜRDÉS	No bathing
TILOS A PARKOLÁS	No parking
TILOS A BEMENET	No entry
TILOS AZ ÁTJÁRÁS	No trespassing
TILOS AZ ÁTKELÉS	No pedestrians
TOLNI	Push
TŰZJELZŐ	Fire alarm
ÚTJAVÍTÁS	Road works
ÚTKERESZTEZÉS	Crossroads
ÚTSZŰKÜLET	Road narrows
ÜDÍTŐ ITALOK	Refreshments
ÜRÍTÉS	Collection (mail)
VASÁR- ÉS ÜNNEPNAP	Sundays and holidays
VASÚTI ÁTJÁRÓ	Level crossing
VÁGÁNY	Platform
VÁM	Customs
VÁRÓTEREM	Waiting room
VESZÉLYES	Danger
VESZÉLYES KANYAR	Winding road
VEVŐSZOLGÁLAT	Customer service
VÉGE	End (of divided highway)
VÉSZFÉK	Emergency brake
VÉSZKIJÁRAT	Emergency exit
VIGYÁZZ	Caution

VISSZAJÁRÓ PÉNZ	Returned coins
ZÁRVA	Closed
ZUHANY	Showers
ZSÁKUTCA	Dead end

ABBREVIATIONS

ÁB	Állami Biztosító	State Insurance Company
áfa	általános forgalmi adó	value added tax
BKV	Budapesti Közlekedési Vállalat	Budapest Public Transport Company
BP.	Budapest	Budapest
C	celsius	centigrade
db	darab	piece, item
de.	délelőtt	in the morning
du.	délután	in the afternoon
em.	emelet	floor, storey
fill.	fillér	fillér
fszt.	földszint	ground floor
Ft	forint	forint
h	óra	hour
HUF	forint	Hungarian Forint
kg	kiló	kilogram
kft.	korlátolt felelősségű társaság	limited company
krt.	körút	belt (street)
km	kilométer	kilometer
m	méter	meter
MÁV	Magyar Államvasutak	Hungarian State Railroad
MK	Magyar Köztársaság	Republic of Hungary
OTP	Országos Takarékpénztár	National Savings Bank
pu	pályaudvar	railroad station
Rt.	részvénytársaság	joint-stock company; corporation
u.	utca	street
WC	vécé	toilet, lavatory

NUMBERS

Cardinal numbers

0	**nulla**	nool-loh
1	**egy**	edj
2	**kettő**	ket-töh
3	**három**	haa-rom
4	**négy**	naidj
5	**öt**	öt
6	**hat**	hot
7	**hét**	hait
8	**nyolc**	njolts
9	**kilenc**	kee-lents
10	**tíz**	teez
11	**tizenegy**	teez-en-edj
12	**tizenkettő**	teez-en-ket-töh
13	**tizenhárom**	teez-en-haa-rom
14	**tizennégy**	teez-en-naidj
15	**tizenöt**	teez-en-öt
16	**tizenhat**	teez-en-hot
17	**tizenhét**	teez-en-hait
18	**tizennyolc**	teez-en-njolts
19	**tizenkilenc**	teez-en-kee-lents
20	**húsz**	hoos
21	**huszonegy**	hoos-on-edj
22	**huszonkettő**	hoos-on-ket-töh
23	**huszonhárom**	hoos-on-haa-rom
24	**huszonnégy**	hoos-on-naidj
25	**huszonöt**	hoos-on-öt
30	**harminc**	hor-mints
35	**harmincöt**	hor-mints-öt
36	**harminchat**	hor-mints-hot
37	**harminchét**	hor-mints-hait
38	**harmincnyolc**	hor-mints-njolts
39	**harminckilenc**	hor-mints-kee-lents
40	**negyven**	nedj-ven
41	**negyvenegy**	nedj-ven-edj
50	**ötven**	öt-ven
51	**ötvenegy**	öt-ven-edj
60	**hatvan**	hot-von
61	**hatvanegy**	hot-von-edj
70	**hetven**	het-ven
71	**hetvenegy**	het-ven-edj

80	**nyolcvan**	njol-tsvon
81	**nyolcvanegy**	njol-tsvon-edj
90	**kilencven**	kee-lents-ven
91	**kilencvenegy**	kee-lents-ven-edj
100	**száz**	saaz
101	**százegy**	saaz-edj
102	**százkettő**	saaz-ket-töh
125	**százhuszonöt**	saaz-hoos-on-öt
150	**százötven**	saaz-öt-ven
175	**százhetvenöt**	saaz-het-ven-öt
200	**kétszáz**	kait-saaz
250	**kétszázötven**	kait-saaz-öt-ven
300	**háromszáz**	haa-rom-saaz
400	**négyszáz**	naidj-saaz
500	**ötszáz**	öt-saaz
700	**hétszáz**	hait-saaz
1.000	**ezer**	eh-zer
1.100	**ezerszáz**	eh-zer-saaz
2.000	**kétezer**	kait-eh-zer
5.000	**ötezer**	öt-eh-zer
10.000	**tízezer**	teez-eh-zer
100.000	**százezer**	saaz-eh-zer
1.000.000	**egymillió**	edj-mil-lee-ow

Ordinal numbers

1st	**első**	el-shöh
2nd	**második**	maash-ow-dik
3rd	**harmadik**	horm-ow-dik
4th	**negyedik**	nedj-eh-dik
5th	**ötödik**	öt-öh-dik
6th	**hatodik**	hot-ow-dik
7th	**hetedik**	het-eh-dik
8th	**nyolcadik**	njolts-oh-dik
9th	**kilencedik**	keel-ents-eh-dik
10th	**tizedik**	teez-eh-dik
11th	**tizenegyedik**	teez-en-edj-eh-dik
12th	**tizenkettedik**	teez-en-ket-teh-dik
13th	**tizenharmadik**	teez-en-horm-ow-dik
14th	**tizennegyedik**	teez-en-nedj-eh-dik
15th	**tizenötödik**	teez-en-öt-öh-dik
20th	**huszadik**	hoos-oh-dik
100th	**századik**	saaz-oh-dik
1.000th	**ezredik**	ez-reh-dik

TIME

What time is it?	**Hány óra van?**
	haanj ow-roh-von?
It's ...	**... van**
	... von
one o'clock	**egy óra**
	edj ow-roh
two o'clock	**két óra**
	kait ow-roh
three o'clock	**három óra**
	haa-rom ow-roh
four o'clock	**négy óra**
	naidj ow-roh
in the morning	**reggel**
	regh-ghel
in the afternoon	**délután**
	dail-oot-aan
in the evening	**este**
	esh-teh
at night	**éjjel**
	ey-yel
It's ...	**... van**
	... von
noon	**dél**
	dail
midnight	**éjfél**
	ey-fail
five past five	**öt perccel múlt öt**
	öt perts-tsel moolt öt
ten past five	**tíz perccel múlt öt**
	teez perts-tsel moolt öt
a quarter past five (quarter of six)	**negyed hat** nedj-ed hot
twenty past five	**húsz perccel múlt öt**
	hoos perts-tsel moolt öt
half past five (half of six)	**fél hat** fail hot
twenty to six	**húsz perc múlva hat**
	hoos perts mool-voh hot
a quarter to six (three quarters of six)	**háromnegyed hat** haar-om-nedjed hot
ten to six	**tíz perc múlva hat**
	teez perts mool-voh hot

five to six	**öt perc múlva hat**
	öt perts mool-voh hot
At what time	**Hány órakor ...**
(Does the train leave)?	**(indul a vonat)?**
	Haanj owr-oh-kor ...
	(een-dool aw vow-not)?
At ...	**...-kor**
	...-kowr
13.00	**tizenhárom óra**
	teez-en-haar-om owr-oh
14.05	**tizennégy óra öt perc**
	teez-en-naidj owr-oh öt perts
15.10	**tizenöt óra tíz perc**
	teez-en-öt owr-oh teez perts
16.15	**tizenhat óra tizenöt perc**
	teez-en-hot owr-oh teez-en-öt perts
17.20	**tizenhét óra húsz perc**
	teez-en-hait owr-oh hoos perts
18.25	**tizennyolc óra huszonöt perc**
	teez-en-njolts owr-oh hoos-on-öt perts
19.30	**tizenkilenc óra harminc perc**
	teez-en-kee-lents owr-oh hor-mints perts
20.35	**húsz óra harmincöt perc**
	hoos owr-oh hor-mints-öt perts
21.40	**huszonegy óra negyven perc**
	hoos-on-edj owr-oh nedj-ven perts
22.45	**huszonkét óra negyvenöt perc**
	hoos-on-kait owr-oh nedj-ven-öt perts
23.50	**huszonhárom óra ötven perc**
	hoos-on-haar-om owr-oh öt-ven perts
0.55	**nulla óra ötvenöt perc**
	nool-loh owr-oh öt-ven-öt perts
in ten minutes	**tíz perc múlva**
	teez perts mool-voh
in a quarter of an hour	**negyed óra múlva**
	neh-djed owr-oh mool-voh
in half an hour	**fél óra múlva**
	fail owr-oh mool-voh

in three quarters of an hour	**háromnegyed óra múlva** haar-om-neh-djed owr-oh mool-voh

DAYS

Monday	**hétfő** hait-föh
Tuesday	**kedd** kedd
Wednesday	**szerda** ser-doh
Thursday	**csütörtök** choot-ör-tök
Friday	**péntek** pain-tek
Saturday	**szombat** som-bot
Sunday	**vasárnap** vosh-aar-nop
last Monday	**múlt hétfőn** moolt hait-fön
next Tuesday	**jövő kedden** yöh-item kedd-en
on Wednesday	**szerdán** ser-dohn
on Thursdays	**minden csütörtökön** meen-den choot-ör-tök-ön
until Friday	**péntekig** pain-tek-eeg
before Saturday	**szombat előtt** som-bot eh-löt
after Sunday	**vasárnap után** vosh-aar-nop oot-aan
the day before yesterday	**tegnapelőtt** tegh-nop-eh-löt
two days ago	**két nappal ezelőtt** kait nop-pol ez-eh-löt
yesterday	**tegnap** tegh-nop
yesterday morning	**tegnap reggel** tegh-nop regh-ghel

yesterday afternoon	**tegnap délután**
	tegh-nop dail-oot-aan
last night	**tegnap este**
	tegh-nop esh-teh
today	**ma**
	moh
this morning	**ma reggel**
	moh regh-ghel
this afternoon	**ma délután**
	moh dail-oot-aan
tonight	**ma este**
	moh esh-teh
tomorrow	**holnap**
	hol-nop
tomorrow morning	**holnap reggel**
	hol-nop regh-ghel
tomorrow afternoon	**holnap délután**
	hol-nop dail-oot-aan
tomorrow evening	**holnap este**
	hol-nop esh-teh
tomorrow night	**holnap éjjel**
	hol-nop ey-yel
the day after tomorrow	**holnaputánin**
	hol-nop-oot-aan

MONTH AND DATES

January	**január**
	yon-ooh-aar
February	**február**
	feb-rooh-aar
March	**március**
	maar-tsee-oosh
April	**április**
	aap-ree-lish
May	**május**
	maay-oosh
June	**június**
	yoon-eeh-oosh
July	**július**
	yool-yoosh
August	**augusztus**
	ah-ooh-goos-toosh

September	**szeptember**
	sep-tem-ber
October	**október**
	ok-tow-ber
November	**november**
	noh-vem-ber
December	**december**
	deh-tsem-ber
in January	**januárban**
	yon-ooh-aar-bon
until February	**februárig**
	feb-rooh-aar-eeg
before March	**március előtt**
	maar-tsee-oosh eh-löt
after April	**április után**
	aap-ree-lish oot-aan
during May	**május folyamán**
	maah-yoosh fowy-oh-maan
not until June	**csak május után**
	chok maah-yoosh oot-aan
at the beginning of July	**július elején**
	yoo-lee-oosh eh-leh-yeh
in the middle of August	**augusztus közepén**
	ah-ooh-goos-toosh köz-eh-pain
at the end of September	**szeptember végén**
	sep-tem-ber vaig-ain
last month	**a múlt hónapban**
	aw moolt hown-opban
this month	**ebben a hónapban**
	eb-ben aw hown-op-bahn
next month	**a jövő hónapban**
	aw yöh-vöh hown-op-bahn
in spring	**tavasszal**
	tovos-sol
in summer	**nyáron**
	njaar-on
in autumn	**ősszel**
	ös-sel
in winter	**télen**
	tail-en
this year	**az idén**
	oz eed-ain
last year	**tavaly**
	tov-oy

next year	**jövőre**
	yöh-vöh-reh
in 1995	**ezerkilencszázkilencvenötben**
	eh-zer-keel-ents-saazkeel-ents-ven-öt-ben
in 1998	**ezerkilencszázkilencvennyolc-ban**
	eh-zer-keel-ents-saaz-keel-ents-ven-njowlts-bon
in 2000	**kétezerben**
	kait-eh-zer-ben
What is the date today?	**Hányadika van ma?**
	haanj-odeek-oh von moh?
It's the 6th of March	**Március hatodika**
	maar-tsee-cosh hotow-deek-oh
It's the 12th of April	**Április tizenkettedike**
	aap-reel-ish teez-en-ket-teh-dee-keh
It's the 21st of August	**Augusztus huszonegyedike**
	oh-ooh-goost-oosh hoos-on-edj-eh-dee-keh

Public holidays

Unless otherwise specified, offices, shops and schools are closed on these days.

1 January	**újév**	New Year's Day
15 March	**március tizen-ötödike**	(Memorial Day of the 1848 Revolution)
***	**húsvét hétfő**	Easter Monday
1 May	**május elseje**	Labor Day
***	**pünkösd hétfő**	Whit Monday
20 August	**Szent István napja**	Saint Stephen's Day
23 October	**október huszon-harmadika**	(Memorial Day of the 1956 Revolution)
24 December	**szenteste**	Christmas Eve (half day)
25 December	**karácsony első napja**	Christmas Day
26 December	**karácsony má-sodik napja**	Boxing Day

COUNTRIES AND NATIONALITIES

Countries

Australia	**Ausztrália** Ah-oost-rah-lee-oh
Austria	**Ausztria** Ah-oost-ree-oh
Belgium	**Belgium** Bel-ghee-oom
Britain	**Nagy-Britannia** Nodj-Breet-on-nee-oh
Canada	**Kanada** Koh-noh-doh
Czech and Slovak Republic	**Cseh és Szlovák Köztársaság** Chek-aish slow-vaak köz-taar-sha-shog
East Africa	**Kelet-Afrika** Kel-et-Of-ree-koh
Ireland	**Írország** Ee-owr-sawg
England	**Anglia** Ong-lee-oh
France	**Franciaország** Fron-tsee-oh-owr-saag
Germany	**Németország** Naim-et-owr-saag
Greece	**Görögország** Gör-ög-owr-saag
Hungary	**Magyarország** Modj-owr-owr-saag
India	**India** Een-dee-oh
Italy	**Olaszország** Owl-os-owr-saag
Luxembourg	**Luxemburg** Look-sen-boorgh
Netherlands, The	**Hollandia** Hol-lon-dee-oh
New Zealand	**Új Zéland** Ooy zeh-lond
Northern Ireland	**Észak-Írország** Ais-ok-Eer-owrt-saag

Pakistan	**Pakisztán**
	Pok-eest-aan
Poland	**Lengyelország**
	Len-djel-owr-saag
Portugal	**Portugália**
	Por-too-gaal-eeh-oh
Scotland	**Skócia**
	Shkow-tsee-oh
South Africa	**Dél-Afrika**
	Dail-Of-reek-oh
Spain	**Spanyolország**
	Shponj-owl-owr-saag
Switzerland	**Svájc**
	Shvaayts
to/for Switzerland	**Svájcba**
	Shvaayts-boh
in Switzerland	**Svájcban**
	Shvaayts-bon
United States	**Egyesült Államok**
	Edj-eh-shoolt Aal-lom-ok
USSR	**Szovjetunió**
	Sov-yet-oon-eeh-oh
Wales	**Wales**
	Vails
West Indies	**Nyugat-India**
	Njoog-ot-Een-dee-oh
Yugoslavia	**Jugoszlávia**
	Yoo-gow-slaa-vee-oh

Nationalities

American	**amerikai**
	om-eh-ree-ko-eeh
Australian	**ausztrál**
	ah-oos-traal
British	**brit**
	breet
Canadian	**kanadai**
	koh-noh-doh-eeh
East African	**kelet-afrikai**
	kelet-of-ree-koh-eeh
English	**angol**
	on-gowl

Hungarian	**magyar**
	mo-djor
Indian	**indiai**
	een-dee-oh-eeh
Irish	**ír**
	eer
a New Zealander	**új-zélandi**
	ooy-zeh-lond-eeh
a Pakistani	**pakisztáni**
	pok-eeh-staan-eeh
Scotsman	**skót**
	shkowt
South African	**dél-afrikai**
	dail-of-ree-koh-eeh
Welsh	**walesi**
	vel-see
West Indian	**nyugat-indiai**
	njoog-ot-een-dee-oh-eeh

DEPARTMENT STORE GUIDE

Ajándék	Gifts
Alagsor	Basement
Ágynemű	Bedding, linen
Barkácsrészleg	Do-it-yourself
Bizsu	Jewellery
Bor	Wines
Bőráruk	Leather goods
Büfé	Snack bar
Bútor	Furniture
Cipőosztály	Shoes
Csemege	Delicatessen
Dohányáruk	Tobacco, cigarettes
Edény	Household goods
Elektromos cikkek	Electric appliances
Elektronikai cikkek	Electronics
Első	First
Emelet	Floor
Édesség	Sweets
Élelmiszer	Food
Felvágottak	Cold meats
Felvilágosítás	Information
Felvonó	Elevator

Férfi divat	Menswear
Fodrász	Hairdresser
Fonál	Wool
Fotó	Photography
Földszint	Ground floor, Street level
Gyermekosztály	Children's department
Gyermekruha	Children's clothes
Gyümölcs	Fresh fruit
Hanglemezek	Records
Harisnya	Stockings
Harmadik	Third
Háztartási cikkek	Toiletries
Hentesáru	Fresh meat
Hírlap	Newspapers
Illatszer	Perfumery, toiletries
Ing	Shirts
Italok	Spirits, liquors (wine/beer)
Játék	Toys
Kalap	Millinery
Kemping	Campsite
Kenyér	Bread
Konyhabútor	Kitchen furniture
Konzerv	Preserves
Kozmetika	Cosmetics
Könyv	Books
Kötöttáru	Knitwear
Lakberendezés	Curtain, etc.
Lámpa, csillár	Lamps
Második	Second
Méteráru	Fabrics, drapery
Mirelit	Frozen food
Mozgólépcső	Escalators
Negyedik	Fourth
Női fehérnemű	Girdles
Női divat	Ladies fashions
Óra, ékszer	Watches, jewellery
Papír, írószer	Office supplies, stationery
Porcelán	China
Rádió	Radio
Rövidáru	Haberdashery
Sarkalás	Heel bar
Sör	Beer
Sportcikkek	Sports articles
Szabásminta	Paper patterns

Szárnyas	Poultry
Szerszámok	Tools
Szőnyeg	Carpets
Szőrme	Furs
Televízió	Television
Tisztítószerek	Cleaning materials
Utazási iroda	Travel agency
Üdítők	Soft drinks, sodas
Üveg	Glass
Varrógép	Sewing-machines
Vevőszolgálat	Customer service
	Exchange and refund
Zöldség	Vegetables

CONVERSION TABLES

Read the center column of these tables from right to left to convert from metric to imperial and from left to right to convert from imperial to metric.
E.g. 5 liters = 8.8 pints; 5 pints = 2.84 liters

pints		liters	gallons		liters
1.76	1	0.57	0.22	1	4.55
3.52	2	1.14	0.44	2	9.09
5.28	3	1.70	0.66	3	13.64
7.07	4	2.27	0.88	4	18.18
8.80	5	2.84	1.00	5	22.73
10.56	6	3.41	1.32	6	27.28
12.32	7	3.98	1.54	7	31.82
14.08	8	4.55	1.76	8	36.37
15.84	9	5.11	1.98	9	40.91

ounces		grams	pounds		kilos
0.04	1	28.35	2.20	1	0.45
0.07	2	56.70	4.41	2	0.91
0.11	3	85.05	6.61	3	1.36
0.14	4	113.40	8.82	4	1.81
0.18	5	141.75	11.02	5	2.27
0.21	6	170.10	13.23	6	2.72
0.25	7	198.45	15.43	7	3.18
0.28	8	226.80	17.64	8	3.63
0.32	9	255.15	19.84	9	4.08

inches		centimetres	yards		metres
0.39	1	2.54	1.09	1	0.91
0.79	2	5.08	2.19	2	1.83
1.18	3	7.62	3.28	3	2.74
1.58	4	10.16	4.37	4	3.66
1.95	5	12.70	5.47	5	4.57
2.36	6	15.24	6.56	6	5.49
2.76	7	17.78	7.66	7	6.40
3.15	8	20.32	8.65	8	7.32
3.54	9	22.86	9.84	9	8.23

miles		kilometers
0.62	1	1.61
1.24	2	3.22
1.86	3	4.83
2.49	4	6.44
3.11	5	8.05
3.73	6	9.66
4.35	7	11.27
4.97	8	12.87
5.59	9	14.48

A quick way to convert kilometers to miles: divide by 8 and multiply by 5. To convert miles to kilometers: divide by 5 and multiply by 8.

fahrenheit (°F)	centigrade (°C)		lbs/ sq in	k/ sq cm
212°	100°	boiling point	18	1.3
100°	38°		20	1.4
98,4°	36,9°	body temperature	22	1.5
86°	30°		25	1.7
77°	25°		29	2.0
68°	20°		32	2.3
59°	15°		35	2.5
50°	10°		36	2.5
41°	5°		39	2.7
32°	0°	freezing point	40	2.8
14°	−10°		43	3.0
−4°	−20°		45	3.2
			46	3.2
			50	3.5
			60	4.2

To convert C to F: divide by 5, multiply by 9 and add 32.
To convert F to C: take away 32, divide by 9 and multiply by 5.

CLOTHING SIZES

Remember — always try on clothes before buying. Clothing sizes are usually unreliable.

women's dresses and suits

Europe	38	40	42	44	46	48
UK	32	34	36	38	40	42
USA	10	12	14	16	18	20

men's suits and coats

Europe	46	48	50	52	54	56
UK and USA	36	38	40	42	44	46

men's shirts

Europe	36	37	38	39	41	42	43
UK and USA	14	14.5	15	15.5	16	16.5	17

socks

Europe	38-39	39-40	40-41	41-42	42-43
UK and USA	9.5	10	10.5	11	11.5

shoes

Europe	34	35.5	36.5	38	39	41	42	43	44	45
UK	2	3	4	5	6	7	8	9	10	11
USA	3.5	4.5	5.5	6.5	7.5	8.5	9.5	10.5	11.5	12.5

Do it yourself

Some notes on the language

This section does not deal with "grammar" as such. Hungarian is a curious language, unrelated among European languages (except for Finnish, a remote cousin), therefore even concepts of its grammar would be unfamiliar to the reader. No attempt is made here to introduce any of these. What follows are the bare essentials in order to give the reader an idea how this language works by explaining some of the most obvious and elementary nuts and bolts of Hungarian, based on the principal phrases included in the book. This information should enable you to produce numerous sentences of your own making. There is no pronunciation guide in this section partly because it would get in the way of the explanation and partly because you have to do it yourself at this stage if you are serious: work out the pronunciation from the earliest examples in the book.

The length of Hungarian words

The most obvious feature of the Hungarian language is the amazing length of some of the words. The reason for this is very simple: English is an analytic, Hungarian a synthetic language.
While the English expressions "from London", "my friend" consist of two words, their Hungarian equivalents are single words "Londonból", "barátom"; while English expressions "I would like..." "may I have ..." consist of three words, their Hungarian equivalents are single words again: "szeretnék...", "kaphatok...?"
All the meaning carried by two or three words in English, can be "incorporated" in a single word in Hungarian.
In Hungarian there are no prepositions (like 'in', 'on', 'from' etc.) put before the nouns, but their meaning is expressed by "case endings" suffixed to the end of the nouns (like **'-ban'**, **'-ben'**, **'-on'**, **'-en'**, **'-tól'**),
There are no auxiliaries (like 'can', 'may', 'have' etc.) either in Hungarian verb phrases, and their meaning is expressed by inflections of the verbs (like **'-hat'**, **'-het'**).
The length of Hungarian verbs is further increased by the incorporated personal pronouns, that is, endings carrying the meanings of personal pronouns (I can read - olvas-**hat-ok**).

Case

Case is the form of the word which shows how that word functions within the sentence. Case in English is expressed by various prepositions (in, on, from etc.) put before the nouns, while in Hungarian by different case endings (**-ban, -ben, -on, -en, -tól,** etc.) suffixed to the end of the nouns.

All Hungarian case endings have several phonetic variations according to their vowel's character which can be high or low (**-en, -on, -ön,** etc.). As — similarly — Hungarian words also have a phonetic character of their own, the endings they take, must harmonize with the words in their vowel character: a "high" word will always take on a "high" ending, while a "low" word, a "low" ending.

in the house	a ház**ban** (low)
in the garden	a kert**ben** (high)
on the map	a térké**pen** (high)
on the train	a vona**ton** (low)
from London	London**ból** (low)
from England	Angliá**ból** (low)
to Budapest	Budapest**re** (high)
to Hungary	Magyarország**ra** (low)

Gender

Gender is the classification of a noun as masculine, feminine or neutral.

There is no grammatical gender in Hungarian. Gender is not very important in English either, but when we replace a noun by the personal pronouns 'he', 'she' or 'it', we have to make a choice among masculine, feminine or neuter. As in Hungarian nouns and personal pronouns equally lack gender, this replacement is easier — you may even completely drop the personal pronoun.

My friend came from London. **He** is a lawyer.
A barátom Londonból jött. (**Ő**) ügyvéd.
My daughter lives in Italy. **She** married an Italian.
A lányom Olaszországban él. (**Ő**) egy olaszhoz ment feleségül.

Number

Number classifies a word as singular or plural.
In Hungarian the plural of nouns is indicated by adding '**k**' to a

singular noun. The ending of the noun can change however before the **'k'** - (á)**k**, (é)**k**, (o)**k**, etc; see vowel-harmony mentioned in connection with the case endings.

room — rooms	szoba — szob(á)**k**
hotel — hotels	szálloda — szállod(á)**k**
town — towns	város — város(o)**k**

There are no exceptions to this rule in Hungarian:

child — children	gyerek — gyerek(e)**k**
man — men	ember — ember(e)**k**

Indefinite and definite articles

The definite article placed before a singular noun shows that the noun refers to a specific place, person, thing, etc.
The Hungarian equivalent of the English definits article **'the'** is **'a'** before nouns that begin with a consonant and **'az'** before nouns beginning with a vowel.

the room, the rooms	**a** szoba, **a** szobák
the hotel, the hotels	**a** szálloda, **a** szállodák
the man, the men	**az** ember, **az** emberek
the shop, the shops	**az** üzlet, **az** üzletek

The indefinite article shows that the noun doesn't refer to a specific place, person, thing etc.
The Hungarian equivalent of the English indefinite article **'a'** is **'egy'** (literally: 'one') which can be placed before all Hungarian nouns.

a towel	**egy** törölköző
a glass	**egy** pohár
an ashtray	**egy** hamutartó
an iron	**egy** vasaló

Practise saying and writing these sentences in Hungarian:

Where is the key?	Hol van a kulcs?
Where is the luggage?	Hol van a poggyász?
Where is the hotel?	
Where is the restaurant?	
Where is the toilet?	
Have you got the key?	Megvan a kulcsa?

Have you got the suitcase?	Megvan a bőröndje?
Have you got the luggage?	
Have you got the telephone directory?	
Have you got the menu?	

Have you got a plan of the town?	Van egy várostérképe?
Have you got a list of events?	Van egy eseménynaptára?
Have you got a list of hotels?	
Have you got a list of campsites?	
Have you got a bus timetable?	
Have you got a railway timetable?	

Where can I get a timetable?	Hol kaphatok egy menet-rendet?
Where can I get a glass of beer?	Hol kaphatok egy pohár sört?
Where can I get a glass of water?	
Where can I get a cup of tea?	
Where can I get a glass of wine?	

Indefinite and definite conjugation of the verb

All Hungarian verbs have definite conjugation when they refer to a special thing, person, place, and have indefinite conjugation when they don't refer to a special thing, person, place etc.
With the definite article 'a' or 'az' you should use the definite forms of the Hungarian verb (én kérem, te kéred, ő kéri, mi kérjük, ti kéritek, ők kérik):

I'd like the bill.	Kérem a számlát.
I'd like the keys.	Kérem a kulcsokat.
I'd like the timetable.	Kérem a menetrendet.
I'd like the menu.	
I'd like the telephone directory.	
I'd like the suitcase.	

With the indefinite article 'egy' you should use the indefinite forms of the Hungarian verb (én kérek, te kérsz, ő kér, mi kérünk, ti kértek, ők kérnek):

I'd like a telephone directory.	Kérek egy telefonkönyvet.
I'd like a timetable.	Kérek egy menetrendet.
I'd like a cup of tea.	Kérek egy csésze teát.
I'd like a menu.	

I'd like a glass of beer.
I'd like a ham sandwich.
I'd like a newspaper.

'Some' or 'any'

In cases where 'some' or 'any' refer to more than one thing, such as 'some/any newspapers' and 'some/any tomatoes' the Hungarian equivalent will be **'néhány'** placed before a singular noun.

some/any newspapers	**néhány** újság
some/any tomatoes	**néhány** paradicsom

In cases where 'some' refers to part of a larger whole the Hungarian equivalent will be **'egy kis'** (literally: 'a little'):

the butter — a vaj	some butter — egy kis vaj
the bread — a kenyér	some bread — egy kis kenyér
the cheese — a sajt	some cheese — egy kis sajt
the coffee — a kávé	some coffee —
the ice-cream — a fagylalt	some ice-cream —
the lemonade — a limonádé	some lemonade —
the pineapple — az ananász	some pineapple —

(**'Egy kis'** is not essential, however, and can just be left out altogether, but remember that without **'egy kis'** your request will be less polite.)

Practise saying and writing the following sentences in Hungarian:
(As word order is relatively free in Hungarian any of the Hungarian sentences listed below have largely the same meaning)

I'd like some butter.	Szeretnék/kérek egy kis vajat.
	Szeretnék/kérek vajat.
	Egy kis vajat szeretnék/kérek.
	Vajat szeretnék/kérek.

I'd like some bread.
I'd like some sugar.
I'll have some butter.
I'll have some tea.
I'll have some coffee.
I need some sugar.
I need some butter.
I need some coffee.

Where can I get some cheese?	Hol kaphatok egy kis sajtot?
	Kaphatok egy kis sajtot?
	Kaphatok sajtot?
Where can I get some ice cream?	
Where can I get some water?	
Is there any lemonade?	
Is there any water?	
Is there any wine?	

Helping others

You can help yourself with phrases such as:

I'd like ... a ham sandwich.	**Szeretnék ...**
	egy sonkás szendvicset.
Where can I get ... a cup of tea?	**Hol kaphatok ...**
	egy csésze teát?
I'll have ... a glass of beer.	**Kérek ... egy pohár sört.**
I need ... a receipt.	**Szükségem van ...**
	egy nyugtára.

If you come across a compatriot having trouble making himself or herself understood, you should be able to speak to a Hungarian person on their behalf.

He'd like ...	**(Ő) szeretne egy sonkás szendvicset.**
She'd like ...	**(Ő) szeretne egy sonkás szendvicset.**
Where can he get...?	**Hol kaphat (ő) egy csésze teát?**
Where can she get...?	**Hol kaphat (ő) egy csésze teát?**
He'll have...	**(Ő) egy pohár sört kér.**
She'll have...	**(Ő) kér egy pohár sört.**
He needs ...	**(Neki) szüksége van egy nyugtára.**
She needs...	**(Neki) szüksége van a nyugtára.**

You can also help a couple or a group if they are having difficulties. The Hungarian word for 'they' is '**ők**'.

They'd like...	(Ők) szeretnének (egy kis) sajtot.
Where can they get...?	Hol kaphatnak (ők) (egy kis) vajat?
They'll have...	(Ők) kérnek (egy kis) **bort.**
They need...	(Nekik) szükségük van (egy kis) vízre.

What about the two of you? No problem, the word for 'we' is '**mi**'.

We'd like...	(Mi) szeretnénk (egy kis) **bort.**
Where can we get...?	Hol kaphatnánk (mi) (egy kis) vizet?
We'll have...	(Mi) kérünk (egy kis) vajat.
We need...	(Nekünk) szükségünk van (egy kis) cukorra.

Try writing out your own checklist for these four useful phrase starters, like this:

Szeretnék...	**(Mi) szeretnénk...**
(Ő) szeretne...	**(Ők) szeretnének...**
Hol kaphatok...?	**Hol kaphatunk (mi)...?**
Hol kaphat (ő)...?	**Hol kaphatnak (ők)...?**
Kérek...	**(Mi) kérünk...**
(Ő) kér...	**(Ők) kérnek...**
Szükségem van...	**(Nekünk) szükségünk van...**
(Neki) szüksége van...	**(Nekik) szükségük van...**

Important thing to remember: the Hungarian personal pronoun ('**én**') must be left out, and the other personal pronouns ('**ő**', '**mi**', '**ők**', '**neki**', '**nekünk**', '**nekik**') can be left out of all these sentences.

More practice

Here are some more Hungarian names of things. See how many different sentences you can make up, using the various points of information given earlier in this section.

		Singular	Plural
1.	ashtray	hamutartó	hamutartók
2.	ballpen	golyóstoll	golyóstollak
3.	bag	táska	táskák
4.	bottle	üveg	üvegek
5.	car	autó	autók
6.	cigarette	cigaretta	cigaretták
7.	corkscrew	dugóhúzó	dugóhúzók
8.	egg	tojás	tojások
9.	house	ház	házak
10.	knife	kés	kések
11.	mountain	hegy	hegyek
12.	plate	tányér	tányérok
13.	postcard	képeslap	képeslapok
14.	room	szoba	szobák
15.	shoe	cipő	cipők
16.	stamp	bélyeg	bélyegek
17.	street	utca	utcák
18.	ticket	jegy	jegyek
19.	train	vonat	vonatok
20.	wallet	tárca	tárcák

Index

Notes

Notes

Notes

Notes

Notes

Notes

Notes